ELT Review
General Editor: Chris Kennedy

Innovation
and
Best Practice

Editor:

CHRIS KENNEDY
University of Birmingham

D1295540

 LONGMAN

n Education Limited
burgh Gate, Harlow
Essex CM20 2JE, England

Series concept and name © The British Council (registered charity number 209131)

ISBN 0 582 42080 6

Set in ITC Century
Packaged by Aldridge Press
Produced by Pearson Education Limited
Printed and bound in the United Kingdom by Redvine

Acknowledgements: The editor and Publishers acknowledge with thanks the following
copyright material reproduced in this book:
Part of page 9 from *Blueprint Upper Intermediate* B. Abbs and L. Fairbairn, Longman,
Harlow 1993; part of page 37 from *New Headway English Course Intermediate* L.
Soars and J. Soars, Oxford University Press, Oxford 1996; pages 46 and 47 from *Angol
nyelvkönyv, Book 4* Fest, Országh, Szenczi and Berg, Franklin-Társulat, Budapest 1942;
part of page 5 from *Materialen fur Bilinguale Klasse, vol. 1: Around the World: Earth
in Space* W. Biederstädt, Cornelsen-Verlag, Berlin 1993.

The publishers wish to state that they have made every effort to trace the copyright
holders, but if they have inadvertently overlooked any they will be pleased to make the
necessary arrangements at the first opportunity.

Correspondence on editorial matters and proposals for the series should be sent to:
Chris Kennedy, Centre for English Language Studies, University of Birmingham
Westmere, Edgbaston Park Road, BIRMINGHAM B15 2TT, UK
(Tel: 0121 414 5695/6; Fax 0121 414 3298; e-mail c.j.kennedy@bham.ac.uk)

Contents

Foreword

In July 1998 we gathered together over 450 ELT professionals from 80 countries
to share ideas about English language teaching. Just over half were from British
Council teaching centres and projects. Most of the others were involved in
projects with us – as managers, advisers, partners or suppliers. All shared an
interest in seeking the best for our learners. All of us – whatever country we
come from or whatever languages we speak – share a background in the British
strand of English language teaching around the world.

Our 1998 Conference in Oxford carried forward the tradition of triennial
conferences for Council teaching centre staff held in 1992 and 1995. We were
delighted to broaden this one to include other professional networks from
within and beyond the Council. A key feature of the event was the large number
of joint presentations, which demonstrated the constructive and creative ways
in which we work together to respond to changes and opportunities by developing new ideas, methods and materials, and by sharing what's new and what's
best with other professionals.

The Conference focused on innovation and best practice across a range of
themes, including:

- management and quality assurance issues, and the management of change;
- the design and delivery of teaching and learning materials, with a particular
  focus on uses of new technology;
- evaluation – of learning, of materials, and of projects;
- cultural aspects of learning.

This collection of papers is just one of the outcomes of our Conference: further
interesting material can be found on the Conference Website.* We decided to
make this the 'formal' publication, and are pleased to see this book coming out
as part of the ELT Review series, with which the Council has been associated
for many years, and which is now published by Longman. We were pleased also
to secure the experienced editorial services of Chris Kennedy, who is currently
the Chair of the British Council's English Teaching Advisory Committee and
also General Editor of the ELT Review series. We decided with Chris to select
papers which:

- were of high quality;
- would be of interest to a wide range of ELT professionals;
- gave a good idea of the themes of the Conference and the range of ideas discussed;
- provided a balanced collection in terms of contributors and content;
- were in article form.

A volume such as this represents a tremendous amount of hard work by many people. I would like to thank Richard Law of the British Council, John Aldridge and the Longman team, and Chris Kennedy for getting the publication out so quickly. And I owe a special thanks to the contributors whose professional inspiration constitutes the core, and who, with others, made our Conference such a rewarding experience.

Tony O'Brien
Director ELT
British Council

* http://www.britcoun.org/english/conference/innov/newin.htm

Introduction: 'Fit' or 'Split'? – Innovation and Best Practice

Chris Kennedy
University of Birmingham

'Fit' and 'split'

We are all aware of the changing societies in which we are living and working. They are characterised by fast moving and unpredictable socioeconomic and political circumstances, fed by rapid technological advance. We are part of a process of rapidly embedding economic and cultural globalisation, with the spread of cross-national corporations, with changing lifestyles and work patterns affecting people world-wide. We are seeing a merging of social groups, but an increasing social divisiveness between the larger groups created. A complex mix of centralised dominance and decentralised group and individual influence results in a constant interplay and struggle between top down and bottom up power. We inhabit a world of neo-Darwinian determinism, yet one in which we have, perhaps more than ever before, individual choice and control over what we do and how we think.

The world is an uncertain and chaotic place, and the social, political, economic and cultural systems in which our personal and professional lives operate are constantly shifting. Sometimes these systems work together ('fit'), and we experience stability, (not always a good thing if the stability represents fossilisation), or relatively smooth change. At other times, sometimes inevitably and not always in a negative sense, systems clash or divide ('split') and we have unstable, disorienting change. One of the challenges of innovation and best practice in any area of activity must be the successful management of these dichotomies of fit and split if we are to achieve the sustained improvement that is the objective of change.

Relevance to ELT

What has this to do with ELT, and specifically with this collection? The same concern with fit and split is evident, although expressed in different ways, in all the articles in this collection. Holliday, for example, has a specific term for it ('cultural continuity'), and both he and Bray and Luxon suggest ways of avoiding potential 'insider/outsider' splits in curriculum innovation. Crystal, from the point of view of the sociolinguist, and Medgyes, writing as a methodologist, are concerned with splits between language behaviour outside the classroom and within it. Clegg and Brewster suggest ways of achieving a fit between language and content.

ELT, then, is not isolated from the social, economic and political developments I have noted above. ELT is part of them, and influenced by them. Operating within a particular sociopolitical framework, government decisions are made at macro level about educational and language policy in international, national and organisational spheres, which in turn have effects on language learning and teaching. Davcheva et al. write of a cultural studies curriculum innovation in Bulgaria which would have been impossible to initiate under the former Soviet political regime. Henry and Pritchard in their article on distance education in China mark the importance attached to English as a result of economic and political reform in that country. The need for English as an international language to be put to practical use in business and trade contexts changed the way English language learning was perceived and led to pressure for curriculum and syllabus reforms.

In these cases, we can see a fit between economic policy, language policy and curriculum reform so that the innovation described was able to be initiated. Such a fit is not always achieved, however, and there can be a split between the behaviour of those using the language and the linguistic choices they make, and the attempt to encourage, maintain, or constrain that use. It is often the lack of fit between policy and practice that can lead to failure of an innovation or to further pressure for change. At individual micro levels, although much language learning methodology remains remarkably unchanging, learners, adult learners in private institutions in particular, are beginning to use their economic power to demand greater flexibility and more efficient and effective language learning (a possible definition of best practice) so that their learning fits their current lifestyles. The use of the word demand is itself interesting – learners are now clients or customers and demand a service, another cultural change that has affected all who work in ELT.

As a result of these macro (national and international) and micro (group and individual) developments, the ELT discourse community, in common with other sociolinguistic groups, is using, as Holliday reminds us, the language of the market, of commodities and of technology. The ideology behind the language, where it reflects a genuine striving for best practice may be a force for beneficial change. In the hands of those with power and influence, however, the language may be used to replace substance by form, and pressurise stakeholders to conform to a particular ideology. This is manipulative change, a form of coercion. Holliday points out the irony of the concept of learner centredness, which if introduced as a set of performance characteristics, can reduce the learner to a product of measurable technology. We must remember students have wishes and desires, and we need through negotiation, to fit what we offer with students' demands. ELT will only survive as an active, forward-looking professional activity if it takes note of these developments, preferably predicting what further changes may lie ahead.

Embedded in these social contexts, is the English language itself, the carrier and the medium through which so many of these economic changes and political developments are conducted. English at present is the international language, and many users express their international identity through using it, raising the question of a new international variety of spoken English. Local identities are expressed through first languages and local 'Englishes'. Crystal poses the question how those setting overt or implementing covert ELT language policy can keep pace with (or fit) the rapidly changing sociolinguistic realities he describes, suggesting that the monolith of monolingual unistandard ELT will have to be more accepting of different models and norms of English. He suggests a new mindset (a split), a recurrent theme we will meet in a number of the other articles. This is one sort of change or innovation (and I use the terms synonymously) with which the collection concerns itself – external sociolinguistic change with which ELT has to fit or run the risk of a split between classroom linguistic norms and standards and the external sociolinguistic reality.

Medgyes' paper has an alternative answer to the question of fit. He suggests that the ELT classroom lives in its own linguistic world, and that we have to accept this. We should not worry unduly about the split between language in the classroom and its application in practice in the real world. He is perhaps suggesting a separation of 'langue' from 'parole' or perhaps that the ELT classroom has its own 'parole'. The classroom is a stage for acting out a play, and we need not worry about life outside the theatre.

Medgyes is here raising, perhaps tongue-in-cheek, problems that have taxed the ingenuity of methodologists for some years, arising from the fact that English language in the ELT classroom is both carrier (or medium), and content, unlike other school subjects which have their own body of knowledge separate from the medium. A partial solution is to adopt a form of ESP approach, in which a subject specialism is created in an attempt to create a fit between language and content learning. Davcheva *et al.*'s cultural studies curriculum created a 'real' subject through which language learning took place. Clegg and Brewster suggest that a language across the curriculum approach (LAC) where language is subservient to the learning of the content subjects, creates a purpose to language learning, enables genuine communication to take place, and engages with the real (rather than contrived) content of the school curriculum through the study of history, geography, the sciences and so on. The LAC approach overcomes to some extent Medgyes' description of the paradoxes of the ELT classroom. However, both the ESP approach and LAC can be adopted only in specific situations, with a number of conditions necessary for successful implementation, and are therefore partial solutions. LAC is generally appropriate in English-medium educational contexts. Clegg highlights the undoubted importance of LAC, but there still remains the large number of educational systems where school subjects are taught through a non-English medium. In these EFL situations, Medgyes' paradoxes reappear.

Some English-medium situations may in any case not present best educational practice (there may be a split between the English-medium policy and the social realities of language use outside the classroom). Such a split may lead to educational under-achievement with teachers and students resorting to whatever measures they can (including conducting lessons in the first language; translation; note-taking and memorisation) to find some sort of internal classroom fit, a form of contingency management (Smith). The ultimate solution is likely to be an eventual change in language policy to attempt a fit. Malaysia changed its medium of education for these reasons from English to Malay; Hong Kong is moving away from English-medium education; and Brunei may have to consider such changes in the future.

Innovation and best practice

I have mentioned several times now the terms 'innovation' and 'best practice'. Innovation is normally planned and deliberate and provides a solution to a problem by introducing some new element. Best practice is a more elusive concept. It implies a norm or standard against which it may be measured. Not only is the establishment of this norm difficult, but clearly the evaluation of outcomes resulting from best practice will vary depending on the viewpoint of the different participants in the process. Teachers, students, parents, administrators may have different views of what constitutes best practice. There are two kinds of best practice covered in this collection. The first is the best practice of innovation, that is, how do we go about innovating as a process to ensure that we achieve our objectives? The second is the best practice that we regard as an important outcome of the innovation, what the innovation is intended to improve, the product of the innovation. In ELT, best practice should result in more efficient and effective learning, and this is ultimately what the writers in this collection are trying to achieve through the various innovations they describe.

Creating a best practice of innovation is linked closely with types of change. Do we want a split with existing practices (radical change) creating a new learning environment in the process; do we adopt a policy of constantly monitoring the environment and changing accordingly so that split is minimised (continuous change); do we settle for getting the fit better, doing the same thing, but better (incremental change); or do we decide that the fit is fine (zero change)? There are no easy answers here. Radical change is necessary where the split between ELT practice and its environment (whether we mean the classroom, the institution, the ministry, or the society) has grown so wide that only drastic measures will ensure a new fit between practice and context. However, one could argue that the conditions causing the split between context and practice and necessitating radical change should wherever possible not be allowed to develop. Monitoring context and practice and continuously changing is one solution, since then we have a better chance of the external environment and the learning context fitting.

Perhaps incremental change or indeed zero change is better? Incremental change is necessary (we want better practice) and zero change may also be justified as we certainly do not support change for its own sake (i.e. without leading to improvement), but they are not sufficient, certainly as single options. By adopting incremental or zero change and not considering continuous change, we cut ourselves off from the external environment which is always inevitably changing, and run the risk of the practice/context split widening. The now familiar but gruesome example in the management literature of the boiled frog is relevant here. A frog does not react to gradual changes in its environment and will not react to slow increases in temperature. There are households in Australia that have to fit devices to kettles otherwise frogs crawl into them, and let themselves be boiled to death, only being aware of the temperature change in the water when it is too late. Relying on incremental or zero change means that external changes in the social environment will go undetected and will eventually lead to radical change that may mean an upheaval in educational systems with all its attendant stress and dislocation. The articles in this collection represent attempts to avoid the untimely end of the frog. They do this at three levels. Some are theoretical discussions of best practice and how we may achieve it (Smith; Holliday); some have an evaluative focus examining new developments in change and how we might investigate whether changes do lead to best practice (Bray and Luxon; Sinclair); others present descriptions of particular projects, courses and methodologies which exemplify innovation and best practice (Brewster; Ellis).

It is often difficult to specify what type of change is being implemented, and many of the articles in this collection cannot be easily classified as describing a particular type of change. Most implicitly argue for change that builds on existing situations (a degree of fit) but one which also pushes in new directions (split) and hopefully begins a process of continuous sustained change. Ellis, for example, describes a traditional methodology which she uses in her young learners classes, but she adds the innovatory dimension of developing her pupils' metacognitive awareness. Davcheva *et al.* build on an existing expertise among teachers of British studies, but change the content to a broader version of cultural studies, and reorient the attitudes and beliefs of the teachers towards a new critically-based interpretive methodology rather than one they are used to which is based on transmission and acceptance of teacher-led ideas. There is a fit/split mixture here both of a continuing tradition (cultural studies taught by skilled teachers) but also a radical change in type of content and the way that content is taught and learned. Henry and Pritchard similarly describe working within existing traditions and institutions, including a specialist institution for distance education. However, they introduced a change in the way the distance courses were taught, which demanded a shift in attitudes and beliefs on the part of materials writers, tutors and students working together on the distance education courses. Split involves risks of course. Sevier describes a radical innovation (though fast becoming less radical) which introduced language learning through the Internet. The enrolment on the course was small. From the point of view of a financial controller, the course would not constitute best practice. However, one might expect uptake to be small with such an innovation, but for it to increase as learners come to believe such learning benefits them. The more we know therefore about best practice in running such courses the better. Sevier describes the advantages and disadvantages of learning through the Internet, and gives a number of principles for best practice which she has learnt from her own experience.

Features of innovation and best practice

The idea of one definition of best practice is illusory (Smith), since all I have been saying thus far points to best practice being achieved where there is a degree of fit between practice, context and desired outcomes. As contexts and desired outcomes change, so will best practice. However, we can at least indicate a number of features, drawn from the articles in this collection, which also tend to match what the innovation literature tells us, that appear to have some bearing on innovation management and best practice.

One is collaboration which is closely linked to the concept of ownership. Collaboration is one of those easy words to use which can hide a reality which is more coercive than collaborative. Consensus building and collaboration may hide considerable disagreement and be open to potential manipulation (Holliday). People may be forced to be collaborative. Participants in innovation may well agree to the suggestions of those in power at a surface level. There will be many ways of subverting the authority at a later stage.

However, a number of the articles indicate that 'genuine' collaboration can be achieved. Collaboration means sharing and owning decisions, and accountability for the successes or failures resulting from those decisions. Collaboration and ownership do not mean that power and influence are equally shared nor that everyone undertakes the same tasks. Nor does collaboration exclude the crucial role of leaders. Power and influence should be distributed fairly and to the satisfaction of all those working together. Different groups and individuals will have different functions and roles and they must have the expertise and support to achieve their designated tasks. If the expertise or support is lacking, means must be devised to provide it, or a different set of roles and functions must be allocated.

If expertise is lacking, this will mean training in the skills and information required as an integral part of the innovation process. Without the expertise, change will founder. Bray and Luxon highlight three sets of expertise required amongst change agents. These include knowledge of the subject content; control skills, under which I would include skills applied to the subject content, e.g. materials writing (see Henry and Pritchard; Davcheva *et al.*;) or technical skills (e.g. computer expertise – Sevier); and process skills (dealing with people; working in teams). We normally assume that such knowledge and skills refer to teachers, the implementers of the change, but students too will need training to reduce the effects of the split between their present classroom behaviour and that represented by the change. Sevier believes students need training in the use of new technology if that is the focus of the innovation. Either that, or you select students already possessing the skills (i.e. you fit the students to the technology). Such training can be integrated with the innovation itself. Sinclair and Ellis show how the tasks completed by learners as part of a new approach to learner autonomy can constitute training by doing. This always assumes that the question of learner preferences has been considered and that the innovation has not become coercive.

In both the Davcheva *et al.* and Henry and Pritchard descriptions, collaborative activity and the training associated with it was clearly important. Central to the Bulgarian innovation was a network of committed cultural studies teachers who were the key change agents and who were given training before the project and during it. Co-ordination and funding was assured through an external agency (in this case the British Council); external consultants helped with training and acted as catalysts for change, and appeared to avoid the pitfalls associated with outsiders; the ministry of education, head teachers and colleagues all provided encouragement and support. A similar collaboration between external consultants, insider materials writers and tutors and institutional support existed in the case of the China distance education innovation. Such collaborative frameworks seem to encourage adaptability and trialability of materials that is also a feature of best practice in change situations.

Acceptability and feasibility are also important features of best practice. Acceptability answers such questions as: Do I agree with the innovation? Does it fit my beliefs and attitudes? Feasibility answers the questions: Will it work? Do I have the skills? These questions are central to acceptance by implementers such as teachers and learners. The zones of innovation that Bray and Luxon mention are appropriate here. Too great a fit between teacher beliefs and the theory underlying the innovation (i.e. almost total acceptability) and there is likely to be no change. There will be no zone of innovation. Too much split between the two (unacceptability) and there will be rejection. One element of best practice in implementing change is correctly calculating the amount of fit and split required. There has to be sufficient split to push the change forward, but not so little that there is no impetus for change, nor so much that the risks of change are perceived to be too great. Assessing feasibility is similarly crucial. Teachers and learners must feel confident of their skills and competencies to introduce the change. If they are not, then, as we have seen above, training programmes are built-in to raise confidence and skills levels. Where fit is essential is in the area of technology use. Sevier thinks that one of the reasons for demotivated students learning through the Internet and consequent high drop-out rates is the unreliability of hardware and software. However much one believes in a change, and however much support we may have had from colleagues, if a change is dependent on technology and that technology does not work, we are likely to lose confidence rapidly.

There is no one theory of innovation, but guidelines such as those described above, applied appropriately in particular contexts, will help to define what we mean by a best practice of innovation, that will lead to successful sustainable change. The reader will find these guidelines implicitly and explicitly stated or illustrated in action in the articles in this collection. However, the purpose of an innovation must also be to create systems of best practice in ELT, for example at the level of new materials and methodology, so that learning may become more efficient, and more effective. Other papers in this collection seek a best practice of effective learning. Key to this search is its evaluation. Bray and Luxon recognise the importance of drawing up an initial baseline for evaluation purposes. If we wish to measure learning progression and the success or failure of practice, we must assess in some way gains or losses between the 'beginning' of an innovation, hence the need for a baseline, and its 'end'. Sinclair suggests ways of developing evaluation instruments to demonstrate the efficacy of approaches to learner autonomy. Without such instruments, the promotion of learner autonomy as an element of best practice may have to continue to rely on the advocacy of its enthusiasts which will not be sufficient for it to become an accepted part of the mainstream teaching/learning process.

The area of concern we have reached here is that of the impact of innovation in the classroom. We know a great deal now about the best practice of the management of innovation, but less about what constitutes best practice in the teaching/learning situation itself. We run the risk of becoming competent managers of the innovation process, without knowing whether the innovations themselves have improved learning and teaching. We may be able to deliver the goods to the correct address, undamaged and on time. We need to know however whether they are the right ones, whether they are wanted, used, and an improvement on the old ones. Many of the contributors to this collection grapple with these issues. Others are aware of the need for this sort of research. Sevier admits that the purpose of her evaluation of the Internet writing course was not to measure writing gains, but accepts such evaluation will be necessary. Henry and Pritchard in the next stage of their evaluation want to see whether their teacher training course did lead to improved teacher performance. This collection has taken forward the discussion on impact and like all processes of change it has raised further questions. Innovation never 'ends' (unless we wish to experience the fate of the boiled frog), and our search for best practice, aided by this volume, will continue.

NOTE:
All references in the text refer to the writers of the articles in this collection.

Prologue: The Future of Englishes

David Crystal
University of Wales, Bangor

The pace is hotting up. Reluctant as I have been to be swayed by the fashion-able neologising of recent years, my title shows capitulation. Like many of you, since the early 1970s I have become used to the steady pluralisation of the noun *English*, in such phrases as 'new Englishes' or the journal title 'World Englishes'. Associated locutions, such as 'an English' and 'each English' are also now routine. 'The English languages' is a phrase which has been used for over a decade, most recently by McArthur (1998). 'Is English Really a Family of Languages?' was the title of an article in the *International Herald Tribune* a few years ago (Rosen, 1994). And I have no doubt that we shall soon hear all the jargon of comparative philology turning up in the domain of ELT – daughter languages, sister languages, and the like. The question we all have to face, of course, is how a concept of 'best practice' survives in the face of such massive and unprecedented innovation. But such a question can only be answered if we are clear in our theoretical thinking about what might be going on, and are clear about the facts of language change which motivate that thinking. Both levels of clarity are in short supply at the moment.

Intelligibility and identity

I begin by exploring the metaphor of 'family'. What could an English 'family' of languages possibly mean? The term 'family', of course, arose with reference to such domains as 'Indo-European', 'Romance' and 'Slavic' – domains where there exists a clearly identifiable set of entities whose mutual unintelligibility would allow them to be uncontroversially classified as different languages. Intelligibility is the traditional criterion, and when that has been applied to the case of English, there has hitherto been little justification for the notion of an English language family. Although there are several well known instances of English regional accents and dialects causing problems of intelligibility to people from a different dialect background, especially when encountered at rapid conversational speed – in Britain, Cockney (London), Geordie (Newcastle), Scouse (Liverpool) and Glaswegian (Glasgow) are among the most commonly cited cases – the problems largely resolve when the speaker slows down, or they reduce to difficulties over isolated lexical items. This makes regional varieties of English no more problematic for linguistic theory than, say, occupational varieties such as legal or scientific. It is no more illuminating to call Cockney or Scouse 'different English languages' than it would be to call Legal or Scientific by such a name, and anyone who chooses to extend the application of the term 'language' in this way finds a slippery slope which eventually leads to the blurring of the potentially useful distinctions between 'language', 'variety', and 'dialect'.

The intelligibility criterion has traditionally provided little support for an English language family (whether it will continue to do so I shall discuss below). But we have learned from sociolinguistics in recent decades that this criterion is by no means an adequate explanation for the language nomenclature of the world, as it leaves out of consideration linguistic attitudes, and in particular the criterion of identity. If intelligibility were the only criterion, then we would have to say that people from Norway, Sweden and Denmark spoke a single language – 'Scandinavian', perhaps – with several regional varieties. The sociopolitical history of these nations, of course, disallows any such option. Swedes speak Swedish, Norwegians Norwegian, and Danes Danish – or at least (as a Dane glumly remarked to me the other day), they do when they are not speaking English. Or, to take a more recent example of how language nomenclature can change (and rapidly): at the beginning of the 1990s, the populations of Croatia, Bosnia, and Serbia would all be described as speaking varieties of Serbo-Croatian. Today, the situation has polarised, with Croatians considering the language they speak to be Croatian, and Serbs Serbian, and efforts being made to maximise the regional differences between them. The 'Croatian variety of Serbo-Croatian' has become 'the Croatian language'. A similar story can be found in any part of the world where language is an emergent index of sociopolitical identity.

That is the point: if a community wishes its way of speaking to be considered a 'language', and if they have the political power to support their decision, who would be able to stop them doing so? The present-day ethos is to allow communities to deal with their own internal policies themselves, as long as these are not perceived as being a threat to others. However, to promote an autonomous language policy, two criteria need to be satisfied. The first is to have a community with a single mind about the matter, and the second is to have a community which has enough political-economic clout to make its decision respected by outsiders with whom it is in regular contact. When these criteria are lacking, the movement is doomed.

An illustration of a movement's failure is the Ebonics controversy in California in 1996. This incident received widespread publicity during December 1996, most reports sharing the content and tone of this *New York Times* editorial (24 December), under the heading of 'Linguistic Confusion':

> The school board in Oakland, Calif., blundered badly last week when it declared that black slang is a distinct language that warrants a place of respect in the classroom. The new policy is intended to help teach standard English and other subjects by building on the street language actually used by many inner-city children and their parents. It is also designed to boost self-esteem for underachievers. But by

labelling them linguistic foreigners in their own country, the new policy will actually stigmatise African-American children – while validating habits of speech that bar them from the cultural mainstream and decent jobs.

The name *Ebonics* – a blend of Ebony and phonics – was being given to the variety of English spoken by African Americans, and which had previously been called by such names as *Black Vernacular English* or *African-American Vernacular English*. Although the intentions behind the move were noble, it was denounced by people from across the political and ethnic spectrum. Quite evidently the two criteria above did not obtain: the US black community did not have a single mind about the matter – indeed they seemed largely to oppose the suggestion, for such reasons as were mentioned in the *Times* editorial – and the people who had the political-economic clout to make the decision respected were also against it. The school board withdrew its proposal a month later.

By giving a distinct name, *Ebonics*, to what had previously been uncontroversially recognised as a variety of English, a hidden boundary in the collective unconscious seems to have been crossed. It is in fact very unusual to assign a novel name to a variety of English in this way, other than in the humorous literature, where such names as *Strine* (a spelling of an imagined casual Australian pronunciation of the word 'Australian') can be found. With just one exception, within Britain and America, there has never been a situation where a specific regional variety of English has acquired a new name as part of its claim to be recognised as a standard in its locality. That exception is Scots. Here is McArthur's summary of the situation:

> The people of Scotland occupy a unique historical and cultural position in the English-speaking world. They use the standard language (with distinctive phonological, grammatical, lexical, and idiomatic features) in administration, law, education, the media, all national institutions, and by and large in their dealings with Anglophones elsewhere, but in their everyday lives a majority of them mix 'the King's English' with what in an earlier age was called 'the King's Scots' (1998:138).

What would Scots look like, if it were written down? A little later in the chapter, McArthur tells the story of a time when he was filling in an annual form which asked him to state his modern language skills. The first few times he wrote 'English' and 'French'; then, as he says, having 'grown a touch mutinous', he added 'Scots' (he is from Glasgow). He adds:

> Nobody commented on the change; perhaps nobody noticed it. But fur masel, Ah'd cróssit a wee bit Rubicon aa ón ma lain – an, efter aa the years that separatit ma faither an me, Ah stertit tae feel a gey wheen shairer aboot ma ain owrelookit mither tongue.
>
> [But for myself, I'd crossed a little bit [of] Rubicon all on my own – and, after all the years that separated my father and me, I started to feel a considerable amount surer about my own overlooked mother tongue] (ibid.:149).

How does Scots stand in relation to the two criteria referred to above? The situation is unclear, because the Scots community does not have a single mind about the matter, nor has it had enough political-economic clout to make any decision respected by outsiders. In relation to the former point, the case in favour has been strongly argued by the leading scholar on Scots, Jack Aitken. After reviewing the arguments, he concludes:

> All the phenomena just recounted – the distinctiveness of Scots, its still substantial presence in daily speech, the fact that it was once the national language, its identifiably distinct history, its adoption (some Gaels would call it usurpation) of the nation's name, and the massive and remarkable and still vital literature in it, mutually support one another and one further and remarkable phenomenon – the ancient and still persistent notion that Scots is indeed 'the Scottish language' (Aitken, 1985:44).

But the missionary tone of this quotation, along with the indication that at least one section of the Scottish community thinks differently, suggests a complex sociolinguistic situation; and at the end of his article even Aitken pulls back from the brink: 'I believe what I have written suggests that if Scots is not now a full "language" it is something more than a mere "dialect". A distinguished German scholar once called it a *Halbsprache* – a semi-language' (ibid.).

In relation to the second criterion, it remains to be seen whether the changing political situation in Scotland (devolution and the formation of a Scots Assembly) will produce a stronger voice in favour of Scots. McArthur is doubtful: 'Any political change in the condition of Scotland is unlikely to have a direct influence on the shaky condition of Scots or Gaelic, because the movement for Scottish autonomy (within the EU) does not have a linguistic dimension to it' (1998).

If he is right, then that eliminates the strongest traditional contender for a separate identity within an English 'family of languages'.

The changing situation

But new contenders are entering the ring – an inevitable consequence of the emergence of English as a genuine global language. 'Genuine' is used here in order to reflect the reality that English is now spoken by more people (as a first, second, or foreign language) than any other language and is recognised by more countries as a desirable lingua franca than any other language. This is not the place to recapitulate the relevant statistics, insofar as they can be established: this information is available elsewhere (for my own estimates, see Crystal, 1995, 1997; see also Graddol, 1997). But it is important to recognise that the unprecedented scale of the growth in usage (approaching a quarter of the world's population) has resulted in an unprecedented growth in regional varieties. Variation, of course, has always been part of the language, given that Angles, Saxons, and Jutes must have spoken different Germanic dialects. The emergence of Scots can be traced back to the beginning of the Middle English period. In the eighteenth century, Noah Webster was one of many who argued the need to recognise a distinct American (as opposed to British) tongue. And the issue of identity has been central to debate about the nature of creole and pidgin Englishes around the world. But it is only in recent decades (chiefly, since the independence era of the 1960s) that the diversity has become so dramatic, generating a huge literature on 'world Englishes' and raising the question of linguistic identity in fresh and intriguing ways.

   The chief aim of McArthur's book is to draw attention to the remarkable 'messiness' which characterises the current world English situation, especially in second-language contexts. Typically, a 'new English' is not a homogeneous entity, with clear-cut boundaries, and an easily definable phonology, grammar, and lexicon. On the contrary, communities which are putting English to use are doing so in several different ways. As McArthur puts it: 'stability and flux go side by side, centripetal and centrifugal forces operating at one and the same time'(1998:2). And when actual examples of language in use are analysed, in such multilingual settings as Malaysia and Singapore, all kinds of unusual hybrids come to light. Different degrees of language mixing are apparent: at one extreme, a sentence might be used which is indistinguishable from standard English. At the other extreme a sentence might use so many words and constructions from a contact language that it becomes unintelligible to those outside a particular community. In between, there are varying degrees of hybridisation, ranging from the use of a single lexical borrowing within a sentence to several borrowings, and from the addition of a single borrowed syntactic construction (such as a tag question) to a reworking of an entire sentence structure. In addition, of course, the pronunciation shows similar degrees of variation, from a standard British or American accent to an accent which diverges widely from such standards both in segmental and nonsegmental (intonational, rhythmical) ways (see Crystal, 1996).

   For example, within a few lines from less than half-a-minute of Malaysian conversation, we can extract the following utterances (for the original conversation, see Baskaran, 1994). At the top of the list is a sentence which could be called Standard Colloquial English; below it are other sentences which show increasing degrees of departure from this norm, grammatically and lexically. At the bottom is a sentence (in this English dialogue) which is entirely Colloquial Malay.

> Might as well go window-shopping a bit, at least.
>
> *Grammatical hybrids*
> My case going to be adjourned anyway. [auxiliary verb omitted]
> Okay, okay, at about twelve, can or not? [distinctive tag question in English]
> You were saying you wanted to go shopping, nak pergi tak? [addition and tag question in Malay 'Want to go, not?']
> Can lah, no problem one! ['I can'; lah is an emphatic particle]
>
> *Lexical hybrids*
> No chance to ronda otherwise. [Malay 'loaf']
> You were saying, that day, you wanted to beli some barang-barang. [Malay 'buy ... things'] But if anything to do with their stuff – golf or snooker or whatever – then dia pun boleh sabar one. [Malay 'he too can be patient']
> Betul juga. [Malay 'True also']

Continua of this kind have long been recognised in creole language studies. What is novel, as McArthur points out, is the way phenomena of this kind have become so widespread, happening simultaneously in communities all over the world. After reviewing several speech situations, he concludes: 'Worldwide communication centres on Standard English, which however radiates out into many kinds of English and many other languages, producing clarity here, confusion there, and novelties and nonsenses everywhere. The result can be – often is – chaotic, but despite the blurred edges, this latter-day Babel manages to work' (1998:22).

I imagine there would have been a similar sense of chaos during the periods of rapid change in English language history, notably the early Middle Ages and the Renaissance. The arrival of thousands of words and expressions from French, for example, would not have passed without comment. Indeed, we do occasionally find such a comment. There is the famous 'egg' story of Caxton (Prologue to Virgil's *Book of Eneydos*, c.1490), for instance (I have modernised the morphology, spelling and punctuation, apart from the two critical words: for the original, see the text in Crystal, 1995:57):

> And certainly our language now used varies far from that which was used and spoken when I was born. For we English men are born under the domination of the moon, which is never steadfast but ever wavering, waxing one season and waning and decreasing another season. And that common English that is spoken in one shire varies from another. In so much that in my days [it] happened that certain merchants were in a ship in Thames for to have sailed over the sea into Zealand, and for lack of wind they tarried at the Foreland and went to land for to refresh them. And one of them named Sheffield, a mercer, came into a house and asked for meat, and specially he asked after *egges*. And the good wife answered that she could speak no French. And the merchant was angry, for he also could speak no French, but would have had *egges*, and she understood him not. And then at last another said that he would have *eyren*. Then the good wife said that she understood him well. Lo! What should a man in these days now write, *egges* or *eyren*? Certainly it is hard to please every man by cause of diversity and change of language.

Egges was a northern form, a development from Old Norse. *Eyren* was a southern form, a development from Old English. French has nothing to do with it – but the fact that the story is reported in terms of French clearly suggests the extent to which there was pressure on the contemporary consciousness.

As a second example, there is the comment of sixteenth century scholar Thomas Wilson, in *The Arte of Rhetorique* (1553), objecting to the 'inkhorn terms' (i.e. learned terms) that were being widely introduced into English at the time (again, spelling and punctuation have been modernised).

> Some seek so far for outlandish English that they forget altogether their mother's language. And I dare swear this, if some of their mothers were alive, they were not able to tell what they say; and yet these fine English clerks will say they speak in their mother tongue, if a man should charge them with counterfeiting the King's English.

'Certainly it is hard to please every man by cause of diversity and change of language'? 'Counterfeiting the King's English'? Hybridisation has been a feature of English since Anglo-Saxon times. Any history of English shows that the language has always been something of a 'vacuum cleaner', sucking in words and expressions from the other languages with which it has come into contact. (This point has often been neglected by countries who complain these days about the extent to which they have been affected by 'Anglicisation'. English has been 'Frenchified' in the past far more than French has recently been 'Anglicised'.) But today, with more contact being made with other languages than ever before, the scale of the borrowing is much greater than it has been in the past. A wider range of languages is involved: there are over three hundred and fifty modern languages listed in the etymology files of the *Oxford English Dictionary*. And the borrowing is now found in all varieties of English, and not just in the more academic or professional domains.

Moreover, we have by no means exhausted the novel kinds of hybrid which linguistic change has in store for us. Consider, for example, the situation which is appearing with increasing frequency around the world in regions where there are high immigration or 'guestworker' populations. A man and a woman from different first-language backgrounds meet, fall in love, and get married, using the English they learned as a foreign or second language as their only lingua franca. They then have a baby, who learns from them – what, exactly? The child will hear English as a foreign language from its parents, but will learn this as its mother tongue. What form will this take? Will there be a linguistic growth analogous to that which takes place when a pidgin becomes a creole – though beginning, one imagines, at a much more advanced level of structural development? What kind of English will be the outcome? We are faced with the notion of foreign-language (or second-language) English as a mother tongue. Our nice models of World English – for example, in terms of concentric circles – will need some radical overhaul to cope with this.

Or, to take another example: the corridors of power in such multinational settings as Brussels. Although several languages are co-official in the European Union, pragmatic linguistic realities result in English being the most widely used language in these corridors. But what kind of common English emerges, when Germans, French, Greeks, and others come into contact, each using English with its own pattern of interference from the mother tongue. There will be the usual sociolinguistic accommodation, and the result will be a novel variety of 'Euro-English' – a term which has been used for over a decade with reference to the distinctive vocabulary of the Union (with its *Eurofighters*, *Eurodollars*, *Eurosceptics*, and so on: for a few recent examples using the *Euro-* prefix, see Knowles (1997); for earlier examples see Mort (1986), but which must now be extended to include the various hybrid accents, grammatical constructions, and discourse patterns encountered there. On several occasions, English-as-a-first-language politicians, diplomats, and civil servants working in Brussels have told me how they have felt their own English being pulled in the direction of these foreign-language patterns. A common feature, evidently, is to accommodate to an increasingly syllable-timed rhythm. Others include the use of simplified sentence constructions, and the avoidance of idioms and colloquial vocabulary, a slower rate of speech, and the use of clearer patterns of articulation (avoiding some of the assimilations and elisions which would be natural in a first-language setting). It is important to stress that this is not the 'foreigner talk' reported in an earlier ELT era. My British informants (I have no information on what their US counterparts do) were not 'talking down' to their colleagues, or consciously adopting simpler expressions: this was unconscious accommodation, which they were able to reflect upon only after considerable probing on my part.

A philosophy of diversity, recognising the importance of hybridisation, does not exclude the notion of a standard, of course. This is a point which the over-simplifying prescriptive pundits of the world consistently get wrong: in honeyed tones, they think that a focus on diversity must mean a dismissing of standards. On the contrary: the need to maintain international intelligibility demands the recognition of a standard variety of English, at the same time as the need to maintain local identity demands the recognition of local varieties of English. My fundamental principle is that we need both, in a linguistically healthy world. And our theoretical as well as pedagogical models need to allow for the comple-mentarity of these two functions of language.

There are two complications which we need to anticipate. First, the emer-gence of new varieties is very likely going to increase the pace of change in what counts as standard usage. It would be surprising if, at least at a spoken level, the trends which we see taking place simultaneously all over the English-speaking world did not at some point merge, like separate drops of oil, to produce an appreciable normative shift. What long-term chance has the tag question got, for example, in its full array of grammatical concord, faced with the simplifying tendencies which can be heard everywhere – and which have their analogues in such first-language contexts as Estuary English (*right?*) or Anglo-Welsh English (*te?*). Would you place good Euros on the long-term survival of interdental fricatives in standard English, in a world where there will be five times as many English speakers for whom *th* is a pain as those for whom it is a blessing?

The second complication is that we seem to be moving towards a global situ-ation in which English speakers will have to operate with *two* levels of spoken standard. This is not something which people have had to cope with before. Standard English, as it currently exists, is a global reality only with reference to the written language: it might more accurately be called World Standard Printed English (WSPE). The comparison of international written varieties in Crystal (1995: 300ff) showed WSPE to be pretty well the same wherever it is encoun-tered. This is what one would expect. That is what a standard is for. It would not be able to fulfil its role as an international (written) lingua franca if it were riddled with regional idiosyncrasies. And, apart from a few instances of litera-ture and humour involving the representation of regional dialect, and the occa-sional US/UK spelling variation, WSPE has no regional manifestations.

But if a spoken equivalent to WSPE develops – World Standard Spoken English (WSSE), as I have elsewhere called it (Crystal, 1997), a regionally neutral international spoken standard, acting as a stabilising force on global spoken diversity – this situation will change. I have drawn attention to its emer-gence elsewhere (Crystal, 1998), having encountered international gatherings where people are using English as their spoken lingua franca, while trying to avoid the idiosyncrasies associated with national varieties of expression. At one international seminar, for example, a casual use of a baseball idiom (*out in left field*) by an American led to the temporary disruption of the meeting (as non-Americans debated what it meant) and resulted in the selfconscious sidestepping of further regional expressions by all the participants. It might not have gone that way, of course. On another occasion, the participants might have decided to adopt the US idiom – using it back to the American, and – by definition – turning what was an Americanism into a global usage. That has been the predominant practice in the past. Whether WSSE will prove to be predominantly American in its historical origins, in the long term, or whether other varieties from around the world will 'gang up' on American English, swamping it by weight of numbers, is currently unclear. But some sort of WSSE, I have no doubt, will emerge.

Whatever the eventual character of WSSE, it will occupy a world which, as far as its use of English as a spoken lingua franca is concerned, will be a multidialectal one. Many of us will have three dialects at our disposal, and – unlike the WSPE situation – two of these will have status as educated standards. Using myself as an example, I already have my original Welsh/Scouse mix functioning as a marker of local identity, and my educated (Standard) British English functioning both as a means of national communication within Britain and as a marker of national identity outside. The scenario I have outlined suggests that one day there will additionally be an international standard of spoken English, to be used as a means of international communication in an increasingly diversified world (as well as, possibly, a marker of Earthly identity, once we have a community presence on other planets). In further due course, the different kinds of standard may evolve their written equivalents, and we will end up with two educated standards in writing as well. To call this situation a kind of diglossia (or triglossia) is probably not too misleading, although the kind of functional distinctions involved are not really the same as the 'High' vs 'Low' functionality seen in the case of such languages as Greek or Arabic. It anticipates a day when learners will have to adapt their British Standard English to an international norm – or perhaps vice versa, learning an international norm first, and modifying it to British (or US, etc.) English. The situation may not be unlike the kinds of shift which learners have to make these days when they visit Britain, and find that the Standard British English they have been taught needs adaptation if it is to work to best effect in, say, Scotland or in Wales. But a world in which there are two educated standards of spoken English seems inevitable.

Towards a new pedagogy

Much of the evidence presented in this paper is anecdotal. It can do little more than provide motivation for hypotheses. There is a real need for empirical research into these hybrid language situations. But it is plain that the emergence of hybrid trends and varieties raises all kinds of theoretical and pedagogical questions. They blur the long-standing distinctions between 'first', 'second', and 'foreign' language. They make us reconsider the notion of 'standard', especially when we find such hybrids being used confidently and fluently by groups of people who have education and influence in their own regional setting. They present the traditionally clear-cut notion of 'translation' with all kinds of fresh problems, for (to go back to the Malaysian example) at what point in a conversation should we say that a notion of translation is relevant, as we move from 'understanding' to 'understanding most of the utterance precisely' to 'understanding little of the utterance precisely ("getting the drift" or "gist")' to 'understanding none of the utterance, despite its containing several features of English'? And, to move into the sociolinguistic dimension, hybrids give us new challenges in relation to language attitudes: for example, at what point would our insistence on the need for translation cause an adverse reaction from the participants, who might maintain they are 'speaking English', even though we cannot understand them? This is the Caxton situation again.

'O brave new world, That has such people in't'. Miranda's exclamation (from *The Tempest*, V. i. 88) is apposite. It is a brave new world, indeed; and those who have to be bravest of all are the teachers of English. I am never sure whether to call language teaching or translating the most difficult of all the language tasks; both are undeniably highly demanding and professional activities (and it is one of the world's greatest scandals that such professions can be so badly paid). But in a world where traditional models and values are changing so rapidly, the task facing the teacher, in particular, is immense. Keeping abreast of all that is taking place is a nightmare in itself. Deciding what to teach, given the proliferation of new and competing models, requires metaphors which go beyond nightmares. Is there any consensus emerging about what a teacher should do, in such circumstances?

My impression, as I travel around and listen to people reporting on their experiences, is that this situation – one of rapid linguistic transition – is demanding an increased recognition of the fundamental importance of distinguishing between production and reception skills in language teaching. From a production point of view, there is a strong case for pedagogical conservatism. If one is used to teaching standard English and a received pronunciation (RP) accent, this argument goes, then one should continue to do so, for a whole range of familiar reasons – the linguistic knowledge base is there in the various analyses and descriptions, there are copious coursebooks and materials, and there is a well understood correspondence between the norms of spoken and written expression (important for examination purposes as well as for reading literature). In short, there is a general familiarity with this variety which must breed a modicum of content.

But from the viewpoint of listening comprehension, there is an equally strong case for pedagogical innovation. It is a fact that RP is changing (to be precise, continuing to change), and that many forms of 'regionally modified RP' are now to be heard among educated people in Britain and abroad. It is a fact that several regional accents (e.g. Edinburgh Scots, Yorkshire English) are now more prestigious than they used to be, and are being used in settings which would have been inconceivable in the past – such as by presenters on radio and television, or by switchboard operators in the rapidly growing domain of telemarketing. It is a fact that new regional first-language standards, in dialect as well as accent, are emerging in such countries as Australia and South Africa. It is a fact that new regional second-language standards are emerging in such areas as West Africa and the subcontinent of India (though less obvious how far these are country-restricted: see Crystal (1995:358ff.). And it is a fact that there are new hybrids emerging in foreign-language contexts all over the English-speaking world.

If this is the case, teachers need to prepare their students for a world of staggering linguistic diversity. Somehow, they need to expose them to as many varieties of English as possible, especially those which they are most likely to encounter in their own locale. And above all, teachers need to develop a truly flexible attitude towards principles of usage. The absolutist concept of 'proper English' or 'correct English', which is so widespread, needs to be replaced by relativistic models in which literary and educated norms are seen to maintain their place alongside other norms, some of which depart radically from what was once recognised as 'correct'.

Yes, familiarity breeds content, but also contempt, when it fails to keep pace with social realities. All over the world there are people losing patience with what they perceive to be an irrational traditionalism. You will all have your own stories of the uncertainties and embarrassments generated when accepted local usages come into conflict with traditional standards. While there are still some parts of the world where there is a reverential attitude towards British English in general, and RP in particular, this attitude is rapidly being replaced by a dynamic pragmatism. If people in a country increasingly observe their own high ranking and highly educated people using hybrid forms, if they increasingly hear linguistic diversity on the World Service of the BBC and other channels, if they find themselves being taught by mother-tongue speakers who themselves reflect current trends in their regionally tinged speech, then who can blame them if they begin to be critical of teaching perspectives which reflect nothing but a parochial past.

The biggest challenge facing ELT in the millennium is how to come to terms with the new global situation. The future I see for British English Language Teaching requires a reanalysis of the phrase: it must not be BE (LT); it has to be B (EL) T. The emphasis has got to move away from 'British English' or, at least, to a revised concept of British English which has variety at the core. For what is British English today? The spoken British English of Britain is already a mass of hybrid forms, with Celtic and immigrant language backgrounds a major presence. Accent variation is always the clearest index of diversity, because it is a symbol of identity: What we might call 'classical' RP (as described by Gimson, *et al.*) is probably down to about two per cent of the population now; and modified forms of RP are increasingly the norm, and regional accents, as we have seen, are increasingly accepted in educated contexts which would have rejected them a generation ago. If you want to hear good classical RP spoken by whole communities, you will more likely find it in Moscow or Copenhagen than in Manchester or Reading. In Britain itself, diversity is the reality. 'Real Britannia: What Does it Mean to be British?' shouted a headline in *The Independent*, and the author (Suzanne Moore) comments, towards the end of a piece in which 'a nation in search of an identity' is the theme:

> The question, then, is how do we create a modern version of Britishness that is inclusive rather than exclusive, that is based in the present rather than in the past, that is urban rather than rural, that is genuinely multicultural, that does not reside in 'middle England' but amongst a society of hybrids and mongrels (Moore, 1998).

ELT policy-making should make diversity its central principle – removing it from the periphery to which it has hitherto largely been assigned. No country has dared do this yet. Even a statement recognising the value of competing linguistic standards is too much for some. Someone once asked me if my notion of linguistic tolerance of English diversity extended to such things as the errors foreigners made. I said it all depended on what you mean by an error. *I am knowing*, for example, is not allowed in traditional standard English, but it is normal in some parts of the world, such as the Indian subcontinent (and also, incidentally, in some British dialects). Would you correct a Frenchman who said *I am knowing*, then, he asked? It all depends, I said. Not if he was learning Indian English. My interlocutor's face told me that the concept of a Frenchman wanting to learn Indian English was, at the very least, novel. There was a pause. Then he said, 'Are you saying that, in the British Council, we should be letting our teachers teach Indian English, and not British English?' 'If the occasion warranted it, yes', I said. 'I don't like the sound of that', he said, and he literally fled from me. He didn't hear me add 'Or even other languages.' For in some parts of the world, the wisest advice would be to recommend that we divert some of our resources to maintaining the life of minority languages. Identity and intelligibility are both needed for a healthy linguistic life. And the responsibility of doing something to try to minimise the ongoing damage to the world's ecolinguistic environment – with a language dying somewhere in the world, on average, every fortnight or so – belongs to everyone, whether they are ELT specialists or not.

There is indeed a radical change of mindset here. To go back to the example of RP. Even abroad, the many cases of successfully acquired RP – where the influence of the mother-tongue is negligibly present in a person's speech – are far outnumbered, these days, by the cases where the RP is being filtered through an overlay of local segmental phonology and syllable-timed prosody. This overlay, as we all know, can be so dominant that it can make a person's speech unintelligible to outsiders. And here we face the crux of the matter. If we observe a group of well educated people from Ghana, or India, or Japan, talking happily together in their country in English, and we find we can understand little of it, what are we to say? Are we to blame the teaching methods, the educational system, the motivation of the learners? Do we continue trying to make their speech improve towards the standard British model (or US, or Australian, or whatever model we are using)? Or do we recognise the possibility that here we may have a new variety of English which has achieved some viability. If this happened in Britain – we arrive in a Glasgow pub, shall we say, and find we are unable to follow the speech of a group at the next table – do we turn to them with a beatific ELT smile, and ask them to speak more clearly? We all know what is likely to happen. The acronym BELT now has a different force.

The assumption, of course, is that if my Glaswegian group were to achieve higher levels of education, their speech would in the process become more diglossic – they would acquire a more standard kind of spoken English, alongside their original dialect. But in the Ghanaian type of case, the higher levels of education are *already* present in the speakers. Any motivation to change must therefore come from their felt need to make themselves understood to outsiders: if – to put it succinctly – they need us more than we need them, then there is such a motivation – and this has traditionally been the case, with the centre of economic and political power lying outside their country. But we know from the predictions of Graddol and others that power centres are ever-changing. And in fifty years time, who knows whether we will not want them more than they want us? In which case, maybe we will have to take pains to accommodate to their dialect (or, of course, language), if we want to make inroads into their markets. It will never be a simple question of code-switching. I chose the word 'accommodation' carefully. There will, I imagine, be give and take on both sides. Trade – whether in products or ideas – is a double-sided notion. But we need to begin now thinking about how such scenarios of mutual respect would relate to our current teaching models and policies. At present I do not think they do at all. I am quite sure that most people still feel that, in the Ghanaian-type case, there is blame to be assigned; that the teaching has been unsuccessful.

I am aware that this kind of talk is controversial. But we have to address these issues. They will not go away. We cannot stick our heads into the sand, and pretend they are not there. Nor are we alone in having to address them. Everywhere else is in the same boat. Or, to be more accurate, they are all in their own boats, each taking on board the waters of diversification and hybridisation at its own rate. American English, with over three hundred and fifty significant foreign language inputs (according to the last census), is at a particularly waterlogged stage, with over a million people now panicking for the *US English* lifeboat (Crystal, 1997: Ch. 5); the last decade has seen unprecedented amounts of water slopping into the Australian English boat; and other first-language areas are beginning to find the waters choppy. So indeed are second-language areas. There is no longer (if there ever was) a nice, neat variety called Singapore English. The only reason we ever got the opposite impression is that, when linguists first began to describe these new Englishes, they were working with individual informants, and their descriptions inevitably presented a monolithic picture. As the linguistic viewpoint widens, following more empirical research, diversity gradually comes into focus.

In my view, the chief task facing ELT is how to devise pedagogical policies and practices in which the need to maintain an international standard of intelligibility, in both speech and writing, can be made to comfortably exist alongside the need to recognise the importance of international diversity, as a reflection of identity, chiefly in speech and eventually perhaps also in writing. English (as opposed to French, Spanish, etc.) language teaching is in the best position to do this. We have an advantage in that our language has been coping with diversity for centuries. It is difficult to talk about languages as *langues*, as collective community awarenesses; but the vacuum cleaner analogy I used earlier gives a hint about one feature of the English language which must somehow be present in the subconscious of each of us – a readiness to assimilate new forms. It is 1000 years since the publication of the first ELT conversation – the *Colloquy of Alfric*, in c.1000 – and already by that stage English had readily borrowed hundreds of words from other languages, chiefly Latin and Norse. This readiness has been with us ever since. It is a readiness which is conspicuously lacking in, say, the modern French *langue* – at least, as it has developed over the last two hundred years. But English has it strongly – and perhaps this feature has been an element in its global growth. As has often been observed, people who have learned English as a foreign language have been known to comment on the way in which they were helped by the presence in English of words which they already recognised as deriving from their own.

Any move to a new mindset is never easy, and some will not wish to make it, for old habits die hard. We should perhaps bring to mind the wise words of Igor Stravinsky, in his *Poetics of Music* (Ch. 5): 'A renewal is fruitful only when it goes hand in hand with tradition'. But there is no doubt in my mind that the concept of 'best practice' for the twenty-first century will need to be grounded in a dynamic linguistic relativism, recognising as axiomatic the notions of variation and change. This is the chief challenge facing ELT specialists in the new millennium.

1 Achieving Cultural Continuity in Curriculum Innovation

Adrian Holliday
Canterbury Christ Church University College

Introduction

In this paper I am going to look at the issue of cultural continuity in curriculum innovation. My major point will be that a major obstacle to true cultural continuity is our own professional discourses which prevent us from seeing the real worlds of the people we work with. We therefore need to be critically aware of ourselves as cultural actors and learn how to see the people we work with in their own terms instead of in our terms.

I shall begin with the principle of cultural continuity and why it is important both in the classroom and the wider domain of the curriculum and curriculum projects. I shall then demonstrate how professional discourses create obstacles to cultural continuity, and how this might be avoided.

The principle of cultural continuity

Cultural continuity is achieved when meaningful bridges are built between the culture of the innovation and the traditional expectations of the people with whom we work. The notion of 'cultural continuity' is taken from Jacob (1996), who is interested in the way in which the teacher mediates between a 'foreign' lesson content and the 'local' orientation of her or his students. However, it can be used to refer to a broader aim which has become common in TESOL in the last ten years – to be sensitive to the cultural expectations of the 'recipients' of innovation, whether they be students or teachers encountering new teaching methodologies, or stakeholders in curriculum projects. Phillipson (1992) and Pennycook (1994) have drawn our attention to the dangers of cultural or linguistic imperialism when dominant forms of professionalism in TESOL are transported from one place to another, as has my own work on how to make classroom and curriculum project methodologies 'appropriate' to social context (Holliday, 1994). The now influential phrase, 'appropriate methodology' was introduced into TESOL by Bowers many years ago (Bowers and Widdowson, 1986). The plea for more attention to the sociopolitical environment of TESOL was made by Swales several years earlier (1980). Coleman's (1996) work on the influence of society on what happens in the classroom is a more recent part of this movement, as is recent

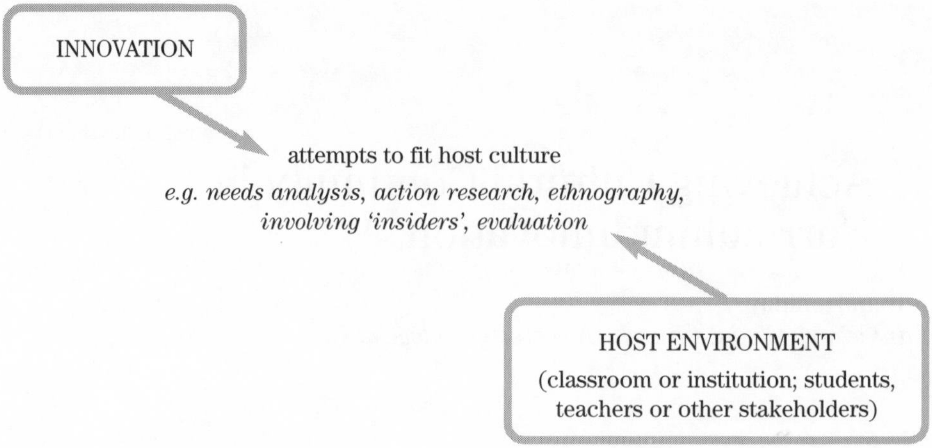

INNOVATION

attempts to fit host culture

e.g. needs analysis, action research, ethnography,
involving 'insiders', evaluation

HOST ENVIRONMENT

(classroom or institution; students,
teachers or other stakeholders)

Figure 1   Cultural continuity

critical thinking about how the paradigms of TESOL professionalism have been
socially constructed (Beaumont and Wright, 1998). The basic idea of cultural
continuity is that a particular innovation is adjusted to enable the best possible fit
with a host environment (Figure 1). It is a two-way process in that the innovation
needs to be informed by data from the host environment.

The dominant discourses of teaching

There is a strange irony here, which involves the problematic nature of learner-
centredness and skills-based education. At first sight, learner-centredness and
the teaching of skills would seem to support the possibility of cultural continuity in that they follow the principle that teaching should connect with the
perceptions and needs of the student (see Sinclair and Ellis this volume).
Indeed, learner-centredness represents an admirable attempt in education,
since the 1960s, to allow students a more interactive, participant role in the
classroom. At the same time the teaching and learning of skills implied that the
content of education had to be useful to the needs of the learner and the environment in which she or he was to operate.

However, with deeper analysis, various writers in education, such as Usher
and Edwards (1994), following the critical sociology of Foucault, are beginning
to argue that learner-centredness and skills-based education might be having
the opposite effect. The 1970s and 1980s brought an increased need for accountability; and a skills-based education lent itself well to the measurement of
student progress through the achievement of discrete learning objectives. The
breaking down of skills into competencies was instrumental in this. The
outcome is a bureaucratisation of learner-centredness. Usher and Edwards
(ibid.) argue that in seeing the student in terms of a set of pre-defined, measurable competencies and skills, she or he is reduced to a learning automaton.
Thus, the 'learner' at the centre of learner-centredness is no longer a real
person, but a product of measurable educational technology.

Two things are going on here. First, what claims to be a sensitivity to the

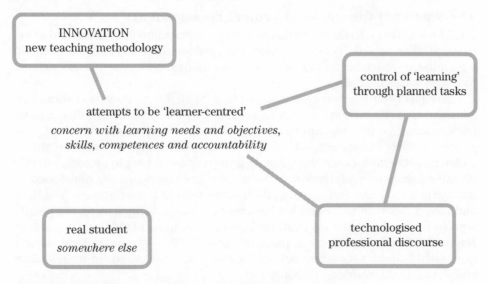

Figure 2 Professionally constructed image of 'the learner'

'learner' – learner-centredness – has become a breaking up of the student into teachable skills. Second, the terminology with which education speaks about the 'learner' has become highly technical. Hence, learner-centredness becomes what Fairclough (1995) calls a 'technologised discourse' which appears ideologically neutral but in fact represents the bureaucratic and ideological needs, not of the 'learner', but of a particular professional group. Clark and Ivanic assert that: '"Skills" [...] suggests a set of neutral technologies or techniques that are somehow separate and separable from the social context. [...] It has led to the viewing of language and language activities as consisting of discrete, apparently manageable and "teachable" components, and so appears to facilitate teaching and learning. It implies a normative and prescriptive view of communication' (1997:84).

This perception is being confirmed in research into the ideological basis for TESOL professionalism. Baxter (in process) has noted that in teacher training programmes, despite the liberal rhetoric of learner-centredness, the real concern is with the technology of teaching, which is presented as ideologically neutral, in which the 'learner' becomes an accessory – for the purpose of accountable professionalism.

Hence, although we might claim learner-centredness, we construct an image of 'the learner' within our own powerful, technical discourse of professionalism. This is illustrated in Figure 2. If the innovation is a new classroom methodology claiming 'learner-centredness', the surface implication is that there will therefore be a concern with the needs of 'the learner'. However, the technologised professional discourse of learner-centredness takes attention away from the real student. Learning needs and objectives, skills and competencies serve the accountability required by the discourse rather than the real student. The outcome is a control of 'learning' through planned tasks, again, serving the technical needs of the discourse rather than the real student.

The dominant discourse of project management

I will now move on to the more macro issue of curriculum innovation and argue that a similar process is taking place. The problem here concerns the way in which the so-called recipients of curriculum innovation are perceived, accommodated and managed.

There has been much recent concern that curriculum innovation should be sensitive to the local setting. This has resulted in what has been called a more person-sensitive process approach to curriculum project management. The *process project* claims adaptation to situational needs. And in what might be called a *stakeholder-centred* approach, groups of local people are quite rightly identified as representatives of these needs; and strategies are developed to satisfy their interests and maintain their *ownership* of the innovation (see Bray and Luxon this volume). Stakeholders can be broadly defined as all the people who have a stake in the innovation. Several examples of this can be seen in Hayes (1997 ed.). In projects in Indonesia and Thailand, Ambrose-Yeoh reports how eighty-seven secondary school teachers are consulted 'in a feasibility study', and in the resulting training:

> A generally friendly and interactive style was adopted to counter any sense of isolation. [...] To personalise the materials and to establish rapport with the teachers, passive language was generally avoided and there was also deliberate choice of pronouns such as "we", "I" and "you" over pronouns such as "they" or "he" or "she" (1997:89-90).

In Malta, Jarvis and Cameron (1997) monitor the changing roles of teachers as they adopt and interpret innovation. Also, Martin and Balabanis (1995) describe how in Egypt, 'working parties' are set up to involve senior representatives from USAID, the Ministry of Education and the language centre where the innovation was to take place, and negotiate consensus. Similarly, Weir and Roberts (1994) describe how 'insiders' become involved in the evaluation of the innovation process, in, for example, the establishment of 'baseline' data, and how formative evaluation becomes integrated with self-directed teacher development.

There is however a problem with this stakeholder-centred approach, similar to the problem with the learner-centred approach which I have already described. As with the classroom, there is a strange irony. As with learner-centredness, a technologised professional discourse has been created. Weir and Roberts (1994) rightly note that as the concept of formative evaluation in TESOL matures, it takes on the role of quality control. Indeed, it falls in line with the growing dominant ideology of late modern society in which everything has to be accountable to the client. Even the process project has to be commodified along with the other aspects of education and other institutional practices such as medicine noted by Usher and Edwards (1994) and Fairclough (1995). Thus, we have a professionally constructed image of the 'stakeholder', as we do of the 'learner' (Figure 3).

As with the technologised discourse of learner-centredness, the technologised discourse of stakeholder-centredness has an emphasis on control (right hand bubble). Here the control is situated in a proliferation of highly technical project documents, at the centre of which are the current log-frame and time-

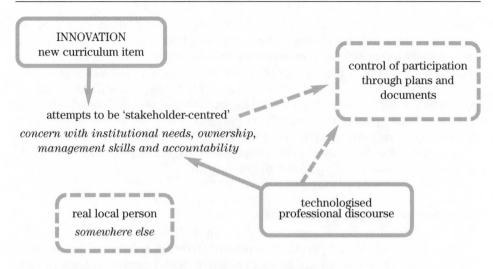

Figure 3 Professionally constructed image of the 'stakeholder'

lines for resource input. Although these documents are, quite rightly, intended as the product of 'agreement' with key stakeholders, they are very much the product of the technologised discourse itself. This is very clear when stakeholders who do not belong to this discourse find them incomprehensible.

In my experience, there is an interesting puzzle here. There is often the *appearance* of agreement between the various parties with regard to project documentation. The hyperrational project discourse takes this as evidence that there is real agreement. Stakeholders coming from different discourses of their own might see the situation differently, and be prepared to go through the motions of agreement for their own ulterior motives. This type of phenomenon is well documented in Holliday (1994), where I describe the operation of informal orders and deep action within the host environment, which have stakeholders pursuing their own ends in their own ways. The following warning by Taylor against naïve notions of mutuality rings true:

> Establishment and maintenance of sustained dialogue between all those involved. [...] [is] not easy [...] There are barriers and inequalities of language, culture and education, and frequently even the need for such dialogue is not recognised by either side. There is unfamiliarity on both sides with the use of common management tools for the sharing and analysis of information (from project frameworks, analysis, tables, grids and diagrams to statistical methods and computer programmes) (1997:116-7).

Something similar was found by Smith (1991) who noted that notions of 'control', 'predictability', 'generalisation' and 'objective' were constructed differently by different parties in educational innovation in a number of scenarios.

An important extension of the discourse of stakeholder-centredness is the equally technologised discourse of evaluation, which bases itself very much on the carefully measured and verified consensus of stakeholders. If this consensus is only apparent, then the technology of evaluation cannot be as sound as it appears. According to Fairclough (1995), a political, though tacit and perhaps unconscious motive of technologised discourses in late modern societies is to create a false image of consensus as we find ourselves gradually consumed by the behavioural technicalities which they demand. As we try to get our heads around the discourse of quality control we find ourselves more and more taking part in it, especially as the discourse takes on the appearance of *inviting* us to participate in our own way. I do not somehow think that the local participants in many curriculum projects are taken in in this way. They have other discourses of their own to get on with.

Empowerment and ownership

This state of affairs throws an interesting light on the way in which the behaviour of stakeholders is perceived and constructed by the technologised discourse of stakeholder-centredness. In much of the literature on stakeholders, there is a tacit power distinction made between those parties who somehow instigate, manage, fund, design, and possess the technology of innovation, and those who do not. In TESOL projects this distinction can be expressed easily in terms of expatriate, 'native speaker' 'experts' on the one hand, and 'local' personnel on the other. This also corresponds with the 'insider-outsider' distinction, where expatriate agencies and personnel come from outside in every sense of the word, and insiders are local not only to the innovation scenario but to the country within which it takes place.

It is important to stress that I am talking here about *perceptions* created within the *discourse* of a particular innovation methodology, which constructs the reality of innovation scenarios in a particular way, rather than the *reality*. It is also important to stress that the writers of literature within the discourse might themselves be unaware of the ideological principles they are perpetuating. Fairclough (1995:36) makes the point that people are often 'standardly unaware' of the ideological meanings which have become normalised within their own language. Clark and Ivanic (1997:176) confirm this when they cite a study which shows that many people are often not aware of the deeper ideological meanings of what they read. Thus, it is the discourse, rather than individual actors within it, which reveals an 'us'-'them' distinction found in the literature.

Clark and Ivanic (1997) make the point that the act of writing is itself a struggle within a world where competing discourses vie for hegemony. Such a struggle can be seen in the way in which Smith (1995) writes about a key stakeholder group which falls into the local-insider category of *'counterparts'* – the people who work alongside 'expert' expatriate curriculum developers with whom there is some form of transfer to enable the innovation to continue after the 'expert' has left.

Smith suggests that it cannot be denied that there may be a power difference in many developing world locations, when the expatriate 'expert' has the 'privileges [...] granted to (or assumed by) the foreign guest' which enable access to budgets, key locations, events and people, and the counterpart does not, and is then expected 'to sustain project impact after the aid has been withdrawn' on

'US$25 per month' (1995:67-8). Discussion of whether or not this is always the case involves looking more deeply at the whole relationship between insiders and outsiders; but here one can suspect that the problem might not so much be one of power *per se*, but of the nature of the technology which the counterpart is expected to carry on. Might it be that what the 'expert' is considered to be *expert* in is not sufficiently compatible, or too ethnocentric to the *discourse of stakeholder-centredness* from the outset? Smith acknowledges that a more 'humanistic approach' to project 'sustainability' must get 'closer to the ways of the recipient' and that the power required to sustain the innovation may not be something the counterpart simply does not have, but something which she or he might 'refuse to accept' (1995:67). Here, as in so much of this literature, there is a concerted *effort* to get to grips with and understand the viewpoint of the 'local', but the outcome, the insistence that 'empowerment' of the 'local' is the answer, is still deeply rooted in the 'us'–'them' perception, in which 'they' 'don't know the technology' and are 'easily dominated'.

Although analysts do try to get under the surface at the deeper social issues, and really do try to understand the viewpoints and predicament of other parties in innovation contexts, they tend to consider large cultural factors as the overriding issue. Hence, Smith puts 'cultural' at the top of his list of 'obstacles' to empowerment. Speaking about Cambodia he suggests that local personnel:

> will have to push hard to bring about any changes. This will be difficult where culturally one defers to and is not assertive towards someone higher in the hierarchy. [...] Others have noted the 'cultural nature of management' [...] and the 'differing cultural concepts as to the appropriate roles for professionals employed in the public sector' (1995:71).

He continues to state the '"need for a thorough understanding by outsiders of the host culture into which the innovation is being introduced"' (ibid.:74 citing Leach). He thus alludes to the model of cultural thinking seen in Hoftstede, who looks at 'the consequences of national cultural differences in the way people in a country organise themselves' and how 'organisational practices and theories are culturally dependent' (1991:xiii).

The rational, systematic nature of this national culture model fits well with the technical needs of the discourse of stakeholder-centredness, as it does with many activities, such as management, which seek to commodify human difference efficiently. Following this line of thinking, Flew sees 'counterpart training' as essentially an 'interpersonal interaction across cultures'. She quite rightly shrinks from the perception of a one-way transfer from culturally superior expatriate curriculum developer to culturally inferior counterparts as 'potentially patronising' (1995:76) and recommends 'mutual learning between people from different cultures' (1995:81). One wonders, however, whether 'trust and esteem' (1995:78) will be sufficient to break the 'us'–'them' paradigm and stand in the way of a potentially damaging culturist process of mutual otherisation. On the one hand, one would not nowadays recommend a professional exchange of views on the basis of a sharing of gender or racial difference. On the other hand, the headings 'training' and 'empowerment' under which the exchange takes place seem to indicate the ideology of only one side.

STAKEHOLDERS

'US'	'THEM'
1 'expatriates, native speakers, experts'	1 'local, insiders, non-native speakers'
2 'proficient in the technology'	2 'don't know the technology, easily dominated'
3 'can: manage, research, plan, evaluate, organise, train'	3 'need to be: trained, treated sensitively, understood, involved, given ownership, empowered'
4 'have the power'	4 'culturally different: e.g. hierarchical, collectivist, uncritical, undemocratic'
	5 'all Indians together'

Figure 4 'Us'-'them' configuration

Overall, the literature on stakeholders seems to create the 'us'-'them' distinction in a very particular way (Figure 4). On the one hand, 'they' are deficient, mainly in terms of the technologised discourse itself; on the other hand, they are classified as such very much in the same way, perhaps regardless of their so-called national culture. One implication here is that the major agent of difference is not the national culture at all, but the power of the technologised discourse. A colleague of mine in a project in India commented that the project created the notion of 'all Indians together'. Perhaps it is not just Indians, but anyone who does not conform to the discourse. Again, an important implication here is what does it all mean if the 'Indians' do not really want to conform to the project after all?

Alternative ways of looking

There needs to be an alternative way of looking at the people we work with in innovation scenarios – in their own terms rather than ours. There is some literature developing in TESOL which begins to do this. Hayes attempts to do this as he records personal accounts of what it is like to be a teacher. Thus:

> One teacher recorded her experience. "When you speak English everybody will (say to you) 'What language you do?' Other teachers (will say) 'You are strange.... you try to show off like this'". [...] It is in relation to their position in society, the culture and traditions of their schools and accepted norms of behaviour within their classrooms that teachers in Thailand have to "re-interpret (INSET activities) in their own terms" (Hayes, 1997b:80).

Similarly, Barmada, revisiting the curriculum project at Damascus University in which I was involved in the early 1980s, reveals an insight unnoticed by me in five years of project-motivated investigation:

> "But sometimes I feel as if I represent the West in the classroom and as if I were telling my students that our methods of learning and thinking are not good and should be replaced by those of the West [...] 'unpaid soldiers of the West'. This made my [sic] very nervous. I should pay attention to what I say in the classroom" (1994:175).

Understanding ourselves

Something else we need to do is to become aware of the fact that what we do as professionals is not ideologically neutral, but that it is part of a powerful, dangerous, ideological technologised discourse. We must come to terms with the fact that our discourse makes us see others in our own terms, and not in theirs. We must not be naïve to assume that technologies of investigation, evaluation, quality control and management created within our own discourses are equally meaningful to other people. We must come to terms with the fact that the bridges we build to reach other cultures might only be meaningful to our culture. The concepts of learner-centredness and stakeholder-centredness are products of our own discourses, and may not belong to the differently constructed worlds of those we wish to reach. We thus need to look deeply and critically at our own discourses before judging those of others.

2 The Role of Baseline Studies in ELT Projects

Terry Bray and Tony Luxon
University of Lancaster

Introduction

Writing in 1994, Weir and Roberts highlighted the potential of a baseline study in meeting the need for 'a more comprehensive approach to evaluation for both accountability and developmental purposes' in which 'both *insiders* and *outsiders* need to be actively engaged in discussion about what is happening in programmes or projects'. They concluded: 'The lessons we learnt from [the] outsider-led, *accountability* oriented approach [...] suggest the need for some rethinking' (Weir and Roberts, 1994:5).

In the light of our recent work in a number of aid-funded projects, we want to take this rethinking on the issues of *accountability*, *development* and *insider/outsider collaboration* a step forwards, and to explain why we believe it useful to see these issues as interconnected in a baseline study.

Since we are aware that there may be various interpretations of what a baseline study is, we will begin by saying where we see it situated in the life cycle of a project and what we think its purposes are. We will then consider the role of a baseline study in relation to accountability. A baseline study is a key starting point.

What has strongly emerged from our work is the issue of the involvement of project implementers in the conduct of a baseline study. The argument we will develop is based on maximising the knowledge, experience and potential of those concerned with implementing the project, and the powerful role that these contributions can play in its effective and efficient development.

What is a baseline study?

The model we present here is just one of several possible models, and differing circumstances produce different variations. Our intention is to capture the essence rather than the detail.

At the appraisal stage of a project the intention of a feasibility study is to establish whether or not the project is worth doing, whether certain basic conditions for its viability exist, and whether there is an adequate framework, including indicators for the measurement of effect, in place. Most usually, but not always, the people who conduct the feasibility study will not be members

Appraisal stage	Feasibility study
Implementation stage	Baseline study
	Impact study
Post project stage	Summative evaluation

Figure 1 Where a baseline study can be situated within the stages of a project

of the implementation team. In this sense, the feasibility study is outsider led
and oriented.

Many of the projects with which we have been involved have had the purpose
of achieving 'second order change', i.e. the alteration of 'fundamental ways in
which organisations are put together, including new goals, structures, and roles'
(Cuban quoted in Fullan, 1991:29). Although the project feasibility study gathers
much useful information, its purpose and scope does not allow it to provide a
sufficiently detailed picture of the project environment needed by the project
manager and implementation team to determine the 'zones of innovation',
(Stoller, 1994), in which these new goals, structures and roles will be addressed.
Nor does the feasibility study normally have the breadth and depth of qualitative and quantitative description for it to be the basis of a properly informed
accountability assessment.

The baseline study is conducted at the beginning of the implementation stage.
It has both accountability and developmental functions, namely:
• to analyse the needs of a particular situation and a particular population;
• to collect information that can later be used to evaluate the impact of project
  activity and outputs at the project purpose level;
• to collect information that can be used to identify zones of innovation for
  project activity, and the kinds of outputs considered necessary to achieve
  project purpose;
• to establish credibility for the project by demonstrating that it is based on
  sound knowledge of the context.

For a baseline study to be meaningful for accountability purposes, there is need
for a further descriptive study towards the end of the project. This is often
called an Impact Study. By comparing the baseline and impact descriptions, it
is possible to show not only to what degree the project purpose has been
achieved and to what degree this has been integrated into the system, but also
what secondary or unpredicted outputs have occurred. These findings are of
importance for the sponsors, both internal and external, since they may want
to pursue the work of the project further, and/or to use the project as a model
for dissemination in the same or other areas. This was the case in Nicaragua,
where an English language project was subsequently followed by a much larger
education sector project.

If the implementation team has conducted the baseline and impact studies, it
is not uncommon for sponsors to require an external post-project summative

evaluation. If such an evaluation finds the baseline/impact study adequately rigorous, then there is no need for much further investigation. If, however, this is not considered to be the case, then a more detailed summative evaluation may be called for.

Baseline studies and accountability

Given the typical three to four year time frame, budget and resources that ELT projects have, we doubt whether existing technology can demonstrate measures of project value-of-output to cost-of-input (ODA, 1989, in Weir and Roberts, 1994:6) when the project goal is expressed in terms of macro-socio-economic impact. Appropriate baseline data do not always pre-exist, and their collection would consume a major part of project time and funding. However, we do feel that there is a strong case for collecting baseline data that can be used to measure project effect and efficiency at the level of project purpose.

Without a baseline study that describes the project environment as it exists at its outset, it is extremely difficult to provide convincing qualitative or quantitative evidence of change. Thanks to the growing literature on baseline studies and better project documentation, it is becoming increasingly possible to draw on suitable instruments. Lessons have been learnt from projects in which it was felt that positive impact had been achieved, but for lack of baseline study data it was not possible to demonstrate this impact.

Following on from this point, we have found that the accountability aspect of a baseline study can be an invaluable vehicle for encouraging project implementers to appreciate and reflect on what they know about the project environment. We have found that:

- *Implementers often know more than they realise*
  Implementers are apt to focus only on part of the 'project picture' – usually the one which is their current professional interest. They tend to overlook other parts in which they also often have experience and knowledge. By providing a frame, which demands a fuller picture, the baseline study taps into this resource.

- *Implementers often assume others know what they know*
  Due to their familiarity with the project environment, implementers tend to overestimate the degree to which their knowledge is shared. What may appear to them to be self-evident may not be so for key stakeholders who hold a much wider brief than ELT alone. This aspect of a baseline study may seem an arduous and unnecessary task to implementers but our experience strongly suggests that this can be helpful in building understanding and consensus of accountability.

- *Implementers sometimes have either an incomplete or faulty conception of what they think they know*
  Some implementers can be so enthused by the prospect of change that they may blame any failure of the project on circumstances external to it.

However, the content of the innovation itself, or the way it was implemented may have contributed to a lack of success. Implementers may be unwilling to recognise this. A baseline study taking opinions from sources other than implementers can reveal alternative views on the innovation and its implementation which can be compared with what actually happened.

The final point we want to make about a baseline study and accountability is that this document is a valuable research document. We do not mean that the findings of a baseline study in country X are necessarily transferable to country Y. However, there may well be salutary lessons to be learnt from its process and instrumentation. Each baseline study in which we have been involved has in some way contributed to subsequent baseline studies in different project environments. Of equal importance is the dissemination of baseline study information and methodology between education projects within the same country. We would hope that ELT professionals see this as an issue of accountability they would want to accept.

Baseline studies: 'insiders and outsiders'

In focusing on the management of change and sustainability, the Dunford House papers of 1989 and 1990 usefully brought to attention issues concerning 'insiders' and 'outsiders' with regard to ELT project ownership and impact. For any project to be effective and efficient, there is a need to set up a communication and collaboration network at a number of 'insider' and 'outsider' levels. What is important is what the project is, who benefits from it and how this can be achieved.

If any benefits can accrue to the project implementers, and the development potential for insiders carrying out a baseline study are considerable, then there is a strong case for them carrying out this work. If the process can be used to build the capacity for going on to implement the project, then it will be useful not only in the products it entails, and what it finds out; it will also help to ensure that people are skilled in what they need in order to implement the project. What kind of capacity needs to be built, and how can this happen through carrying out a baseline study?

Development: project skills and agendas

Although projects may vary according to their aims and areas of development, there are nevertheless basic project skills that are required in whichever type of project is being implemented. Whether the work of the project is concerned with, for example testing, teacher/trainer training, curriculum reform or any other aspect of language teaching, there are certain agendas which have to be addressed. In order to carry out a project successfully, a project team needs to address these agendas to be able to manage effectively. Buchanan and Boddy usefully identify these as follows:

1 *The content agenda*
   The project manager is expected to be technically competent and experienced
   with respect to the substance of the changes being implemented – for example,
   with respect to the hardware and software capabilities and limitations of a
   networked management information system.

2 *The control agenda*
   The project manager is expected to be familiar and competent with a range of
   planning, scheduling, budgeting, resourcing and monitoring techniques, with
   setting and meeting deadlines and targets – the staple fare of project management courses.

3 *The process agenda*
   Sometimes covered under the heading of implementation skills, the project
   manager is expected to be competent in communications and consultation, in
   team building, in influencing and negotiating skills, and in the management of
   enthusiasm and resistance (Buchanan and Boddy, 1992: 28).

As can be seen from the language used and the examples given, the specific
area referred to above is the management of innovation in Information
Technology, but these agendas can be equally applied to innovative language
projects. In a testing project, for example, the *content* agenda might be knowledge of item writing, test specifications, sub-skills to be tested and overall
design of tests. The *control* agenda might be concerned with the administration
of the tests, for example the distribution of tests to centres, security, making
sure the necessary human and technical resources are in place, and the
collating of results. The *process* agenda might cover negotiations with examination bodies, recruitment of examiners, building a team of testers for standardis-
ation purposes, and communications between test designers and examiners.
There is considerable overlap between these agendas, and it could be the case
that certain activities fall into two or perhaps even all three of the agendas, but
there is a difference of emphasis in each of the categories.

   What might happen if these agendas are not attended to? In a testing project,
if there are people who are excellent test designers and item writers, then the
content agenda can be successfully dealt with. However, if the team members
are not concerned with how the tests are distributed, how they are paid for,
how they are resourced for example, then considerable problems may arise.
Likewise, a new test will involve relations between teachers, trainers, school
heads, as well as among test designers, and if these relationships are not
attended to, then no matter how well the test is designed, it may not fulfil its
purpose. Wall (1996) indicates problems arising from the introduction of new
tests into traditional systems and finds that many of these stem from difficulties and failures in communication with teachers, students and schools.

Project skills and baseline studies

Is it possible to skill people for these agendas through a baseline study exercise? Our experience tells us that it is, in many cases, but if the baseline study
were not useful for this kind of skilling, then some other way would need to be

found. However, its place at the beginning of the project, its purpose in finding out about the project environment in a systematic way is too good an opportunity to miss. What kind of activities involved in carrying out a baseline study can contribute to building the necessary capacity for the successful implementation of a project?

In terms of the *content* agenda, there are often opportunities for analysing events or documents in a systematic and critical way which may not have presented themselves previously. For example, during the baseline study for a Ukrainian project concerned with reform of the ELT pre-service teacher training curriculum, the project team had to analyse the existing syllabus in terms of its match with the real needs of teachers in secondary schools. They needed to find out what really happened in the classroom after teachers had finished their training, in order to see if it had been useful and relevant. In order to do this they carried out classroom observation, had discussions with teachers and analysed the elements of the current curriculum. This process prepared the team for the tasks of creating a new curriculum, supporting, supervising and evaluating teachers, and making the connections between college based training and school based teacher development. In short, what they learned through the process of collecting data for the baseline study was then useful for the implementation of the project.

Similarly, in Cambodia, a newly created inspection team carried out the baseline study for an in-service teacher training project. Their proposed role in the project was to visit schools, talk to teachers and students, and offer support, in order to monitor and improve the quality of teaching and learning in Cambodian state schools. The baseline study was seen as an excellent opportunity to develop the necessary skills to carry out their task. Again, these were directly transferable skills.

In both these examples, the capacity was being developed which enabled team members to be technically competent and experienced with respect to the substance of the changes being implemented.

As far as the *control* agenda is concerned, a complex exercise such as carrying out research at a national or regional level requires the team to determine what resources are needed to do the research, how much time needs to be made available, how much the research will need in terms of person hours and financing, how visits can be scheduled, and how work can be divided among team members. In the case of the Ukrainian curriculum reform team, the members made an implementation plan covering who did what, how, where and when, and how much it would all cost. The team had to manage the baseline study using management skills which would be required to run a project. Again, these are directly transferable skills, which probably, before the baseline study, they would not have had the need, the opportunity or even the desire to utilise.

The *process* agenda is concerned with people and communication. In order to carry out such an exercise, the team would have to liaise with ministry officials, head teachers, university lecturers and heads of department, and with primary and secondary stakeholders, however these are defined. In an ELT project in Nicaragua, the baseline study provided the opportunity to establish a communications network among groups of people who would be involved in the implementation of the project, or who would be affected by the activities of the project.

In all of this baseline study activity, there is a strong element of team building. The team would have to get to know each other's strengths and weaknesses both in professional and personal terms. By the end of the exercise, the team has worked together on a mini-project which acts as a trial for what they will have to do over the life of the project itself.

Therefore, not only has the team carried out invaluable research for the project, and produced documentation for evaluation, they have also developed the skills to be able to implement the project based on the research they have done. In terms of *accountability*, they will have certain products, principally a baseline study report, that can be used in subsequent evaluation and monitoring. In terms of *development*, the capacity for managing a project has increased considerably.

It might be useful at this point to quote directly from the baseline study of a project concerned with in-service teacher training in Ukraine which illustrates what the team gained from the process of carrying out their research.

> ### The challenge to the team
>
> For the majority of team members this was the first experience of research work of this nature, involving the close study of situations and attitudes in the real world. While the team acknowledges mistakes were made due to lack of experience, we can identify several gains made as a result of work on this study:
>
> - All members of the team have gained experience in a mode of research which is very new to Ukraine; that is research which is centred around professional practices and carried out by practitioners.
>
> - Team members have a clearer grasp of the issues surrounding approaches to ELT.
>
> - Team members have become familiar with a method of observing lessons which allows the observer to assess all aspects of a lesson, in much more detail than traditional observation techniques allow.
>
> - The groups of secondary stakeholders who are rarely, if ever, consulted have been given the opportunity to consider some of the issues surrounding ELT to express their own views on the current state of ELT in Ukrainian schools.
>
> - Secondary stakeholders have been made aware of the possibility of change.
>
> *(Ukraine Project Teams, 1997)*

There is a case to be made for deciding against a baseline study being carried out by practitioners and bringing in a professional evaluator from outside the project. This issue has been the subject of debate within the evaluation literature. We do not wish to go over this particular debate here, only to say that there may well be a tension between the developmental and evaluative aspects of a baseline study carried out by project implementers who are not, strictly speaking, professional evaluators. As stated above, mistakes can be made. However, the gains to insider participants through the process must be taken in balance with the need for an effective evaluative instrument. To quote Weir and Roberts:

> While we know that the collection and analysis of data should meet the standards of feasibility and accuracy, we have also learnt that positive interpersonal and institutional relationships must underpin technical adequacy, and are at the heart of effective evaluation: this is because relationships of commitment and trust enable the involvement of players in the evaluation process, and the utilisation of findings. We have learnt that the importance of these relationships must be taken into account from the very outset...' (Weir and Roberts, 1994:218).

We believe our experience shows that the carrying out of baseline study research is an invaluable opportunity, not only to provide a basis for future evaluation of a project, but also as the ground on which the necessary capacity for implementing a project can be built, and the case for this process being carried out by project implementers is strong.

3 Managing ELT Projects: Identifying Best Practice

Harvey Smith
CfBT Education Services, Reading

Introduction

The theme of this collection of papers is innovation and best practice in ELT. 'Innovation' is reasonably easy to define – the introduction of something new. The more difficult part of the theme is the concept of 'best practice'. This is difficult because it implies that there is a single optimum way of undertaking something, or that experts or practitioners can agree on what may be the one best way. I shall be looking at this concept in relation to the management of aid-funded ELT projects. Over the last two decades there have been large numbers of ELT projects, yet it would seem that no clear idea of what constitutes 'best practice' in the management of ELT projects has emerged.

It could be simply that this is a sphere of activity to which it is impossible to apply the term 'best practice'. In trying to do so, I have found that there are far more questions than answers. This paper is intended solely to examine the sort of questions which need to be considered – in other words, its aim is to discuss what sort of questions we need to ask, and what the implications of such questions might be. It does not aim to define what sort of activities might be labelled best practice.

Can there be agreement about what best practice is?

There are two major issues when dealing with this question. The first relates to the number of people who need to be in agreement. There is a wide range of stakeholders involved in aid-funded ELT projects – as a minimum, I would suggest there must be five parties:
- the donor providing the aid funding;
- the recipient; the government of the developing country or the ministry or other institution receiving the aid;
- the implementing agency which is managing the project or providing the technical consultants or arranging the training;
- the project team actually undertaking the work of the project;
- the beneficiaries who are intended to benefit from it.

In many contexts the list will be considerably longer. To take one example, in Cambodia, where C*f*BT manages the Cambodian Secondary English Teaching Project, others who need to be added to this list include inspectors, head teachers, teachers, teacher trainers, teacher trainees, VSO volunteers working in teacher training centres, students in schools, parents and employers. Each of these stakeholders can be expected to have a different perspective on what the project is about, on who is benefiting from it, on the way it should be run. It seems reasonable to question whether it is realistic to expect such a wide range of stakeholders to agree on what best practice might be.

The second key issue in relation to this first question is whether there is any means of establishing agreement between so many parties. There is much more participation than there used to be in project design, which in the case of the UK Department for International Development (DFID) projects is now carried out at least in part through participatory design workshops which involve a number of stakeholders. But establishing a consensus on what a project is intended to do is not sufficient for us to be able to say that we are anywhere near a consensus on best practice in the way the project is implemented. While it may in theory be possible to establish such a consensus, I am not sure that we have the means to do so yet.

Who defines best practice?

In other words, which of the stakeholders has the 'right' perspective? (See Holliday, this volume.) Whose best practice is the right one? Traditionally it has been seen as the donor's prerogative to define what is acceptable or unacceptable. The donor clearly has a claim, because the donor is providing the money without which the project could not happen. Although there have been changes in the way other stakeholders are involved, it has also been the donor who has undertaken the major reviews and evaluations. Much of what is discovered by such evaluations has also remained with the donor, rather than being disseminated and fed into wider discussion with other stakeholders on issues such as best practice.

However, the donor is not the only party with a claim. The recipient government or host institution also has a claim, as they have (either genuinely or nominally) requested the aid donor to fund the project, and the project's aims are to provide some support to that government's or institution's policies or capacity. External ELT specialists have a claim, as they may have designed the details of the project and/or are working in the developing country to achieve the project's objectives, and they, as ELT experts, may see themselves as best placed to advise on the way the project should be managed. The headteachers, whose teachers are being trained by the project, may also have a claim, as they have to live with the consequences of the project, long after external consultants have gone. The teachers whose behaviour is expected to change as a result of the project may also have a claim; and so on.

It may be the case that all these parties would agree on what best practice might be. However, until that is shown to be the case, project implementers should assume that it is not, and should be prepared to investigate the issue further as best they can.

Should best practice be defined in terms of ELT or of project management, or both?

When we speak of the management of aid-funded ELT projects, where should we be looking for best practice: in the way aid funds are used; in the way ELT is delivered, i.e. the way English is taught; or in the way the project is managed?

These questions imply three elements in the management of aid-funded ELT projects – aid, English teaching and project management, but there is a fourth. Although known as ELT projects, such projects rarely exist to teach English. A project is set up to bring about some change in the way English teaching is delivered. Are we, then, looking for best practice in the way such change is brought about?

This implies that seeking to identify best practice is more complex than might first be thought. As it is aid-funded, the ELT project should accord with best practice in the delivery of aid. As it is concerned with ELT, it should accord with best practice in the delivery of competence in English. As it is a project, it should accord with best practice in project management. As it exists to bring about change, it should accord with best practice in change management. (I have excluded education as a dimension here, as I believe that what applies to education is already covered by the four elements I have described, but others may feel that best practice in education is a further category with which the ELT project has to be in line.)

What criteria can be identified?

From the point of view of the use of aid funds, the donor has imposed a framework, the project or logical framework, which summarises what the project is expected to achieve and the activities and inputs which are expected to result in the achievement of the objectives. From this point of view, the project becomes a management task of turning inputs into outputs. Best practice could then be seen as that which results in the achievement of the outputs most efficiently, i.e. using the least resources. However, given that aid is intended to bring about socioeconomic development, best practice may also be defined in terms of what practices are most likely to achieve the intended development. This assumes that there is agreement on what sort of development is best and how that can best be achieved – and the long debates on this issue do not suggest that there is yet such agreement. There is also the issue already mentioned that this is a donor perspective, rather than that of the many other stakeholders.

From the point of view of ELT, best practice can be described in terms of what most effectively results in the appropriate competence in English for the target learners. I think we are much closer to agreement on what that might be than we were a decade ago, in that there no longer seem to be new approaches and methodologies hitting the journals and the university faculties of education as frequently as there used to be, and a degree of eclecticism seems to be accepted as the norm. One problem, however, is that projects do not necessarily come into contact with the target learners whose competence in English the project is intended to influence for the better. A teacher training project, for example, may have as its goal improved competence in the English of school leavers – but whether the project's work with trainer trainers has actually influenced the learning of English in the classroom is something which cannot necessarily be established during the life of the project, and there may be other variables which could influence that outcome, so that it will not be easy to establish whether the practices adopted by the project are indeed as effective as was hoped.

From the project management perspective, a project's objectives do not just have to be achieved but should be achieved within the constraints of time, budget and specification or quality. Best practice would then be seen as whatever resulted in the project's objectives being met within the agreed time-frame, within the agreed budget, and to the level of quality specified.

From the perspective of achieving change – that is changing the way English is taught – the project needs to achieve a change which is sustainable. Best practice would then be seen as whatever resulted in the change in behaviour which continued longest after the project had finished.

In broad terms, then, and ignoring for the moment possible disagreement between various stakeholders, best practice in aid-funded ELT project management is that which results in the objectives of the project being achieved efficiently, on time, within budget, to the appropriate level of quality, resulting in improved levels of competence in English in a target group of learners and improved socioeconomic development of the country.

Is best practice universal, or is it dependent on the specific environment?

This is a fundamental question going way beyond ELT projects. It can be asked whether there is a single right way of managing organisations, temporary or permanent. Studies of organisational behaviour using what is known as a contingency approach maintain that the effective performance of an organisation depends on the 'goodness of fit' between a number of variables, within the organisation and between the organisation and the environment. The approach suggests, not that there is simply a relationship between one factor or a set of factors and effective performance, but that it is the relationship between those factors and the relationship between factors within the organisation and the environment (Lawrence and Lorsch, 1967) on which effective performance is contingent.

While this approach to organisational behaviour was developed in the west – USA and Britain – and has been applied to the study of educational organisations in these countries, it would seem to be even more true for projects in developing countries. It also accords neatly with the definition of a project, which is in part that it is a one-off or unique undertaking. There have been many studies using a contingency approach on aid-funded education projects (Verspoor, 1985; Middleton *et al.*, 1987; Rondinelli *et al.*, 1990). As the approach actually starts from the premise that there can be no one best way of managing organisations but that this is environment-contingent, if we accept the premise then we need to define best practice in a different way. Best practice in ELT project management is then concerned with identifying what sort of relationship between the main factors in the project best suits the environment.

In the contingency theory literature such factors are seen as related to the structure of the organisation, its staff, its tasks and its management processes (Mintzberg, 1979; Child, 1984). If the approach is valid then best practice relates to establishing a relationship between the project's structure, staffing, activities and management processes which provide the best fit with the physical, political, economic, cultural and social environment. As this environment differs from country to country and as so many characteristics differ from project to project, it must be inevitable that the actual implementation practices should differ too.

What are the barriers to the achievement of best practice?

The following are general barriers in line with the discussion so far. I am not making any attempt to look at barriers to carrying out specific activities.

- The first barrier to the achievement of best practice must be that it seems to be almost impossible to define. Given all the variables in a project, it is probably only after the project has been completed that one can assess whether or not aspects of its implementation would appear to have been 'for the best'.
- A second barrier lies in the problem of satisfying all the stakeholders. On the assumption that it will not be possible to get agreement between them all, one task of the project manager or implementer is to decide, at various points, which stakeholders to satisfy and which to ignore. As the project manager's salary and career probably depend on satisfying the donor, best interests, rather than best practice, may determine what actually happens.
- A third barrier lies in defining the environment – or, more importantly, predicting what the environment will be like at the end of the project. Whether or not one accepts all the arguments of the contingency approach, there can be little doubt that best practice includes being environment-sensitive. But bringing about sustainable change in behaviour requires a capacity to predict what the environment will be like after the project has finished.
- A fourth barrier lies in the fact that many aspects of the project have been fixed before the project manager (or head of project) arrives on the scene. If best practice lies in achieving the right sort of relationship between a number of factors, it may be difficult for the project manager to influence such factors. For example, the relationship between the donor and the host institution may already be well established, the project design fully completed and the other staff in the project team already appointed. The project manager's hands are to a considerable extent tied by decisions which are key to the project but in which she or he has not been consulted.

What further research is needed to help establish the factors involved?

When one reads the literature on aid-funded projects, it is almost always from the perspective of the donor or of the expatriate specialist. There is very little in the literature which approaches projects from the point of view of other stakeholders. While expatriates, including myself (Smith, 1997) have attempted to second-guess what the perceptions of such local stakeholders might be, there is clearly a need for a more accurate idea of what different stakeholders on the recipient side perceive as positive and negative in the way ELT projects are managed.

A further area is already being investigated. I have suggested that best practice in aid-funded ELT projects would need to meet both the criteria of effective aid delivery, which relate to the extent to which the project results in socioeconomic development, and the criteria of effective ELT delivery, which relate to the extent to which the project results in improved English competence within a specific target group. The assumption has been that there is a correlation between improved English competence and socioeconomic development. The British government's 1997 White Paper on international development has made the focus of its policy to aid poverty elimination, and this has raised questions about the evidence for the correlation between competence in English and reducing poverty. CfBT and the British Council have together been exploring ways of encouraging research into this, and CfBT has funded a short piece of research in this field undertaken by Reading University.

I have suggested that the relationship between a project and its environment may also be important in determining best practice in project management. What the effects are of such relationships requires considerable investigation.

Conclusion

While I am not suggesting that it is impossible to identify best practice in the management of ELT projects, I am suggesting that we are not yet ready to do so. If my analysis is right, best practice lies in:

- achieving agreement between all the different stakeholders in the project on the way the project is implemented;
- undertaking activities in such a way that the agreed objectives of the project are achieved efficiently – i.e. with the minimum resources required; on time; within budget; and to an agreed or appropriate level of quality;
- undertaking activities in such a way that there is a sustainable change in behaviour and they are consonant with the project's environment;
- undertaking activities that result in improved English competence in the target group and in socioeconomic development.

It may be felt that there are other issues untouched here. What about wider impact regardless of the specific objectives of the project? What about professionalism? What about developing relationships which may create other positive outcomes – for example further contracts for the implementing agency or commercial or political benefits for the donor or host institution? What about being able to change direction in mid-stream? All of these are worthy of further consideration (see Smith, 1998), but are not as important as the other points.

If we see ourselves as professionals, then I would suggest we have a duty to pursue this issue, difficult as it may seem. In the end, it is probably less important that we achieve consensus on what best practice is, and more important that we are conscious that we need to try to define it and to ensure that it underlies our decision-making..

4 TEFL by Distance

Jane Henry and Norman Pritchard
British Council, Beijing

Introduction

This paper describes a four year project jointly run and financed by the Chinese Ministry of Education (known as the State Education Commision (SEdC) when this project started) and the British Department for International Development (DFID), formerly the British Overseas Development Administration (ODA). The project is based in Beijing and is a result of the collaboration between the Beijing Foreign Studies University (BFSU) and the China Central Radio and Television University (CCRTVU). Its aim is to set up a three year distance BA degree in Teaching English as a Foreign Language to upgrade the two year diploma held by Chinese middle school teachers all over the country. By the end of the project, fifteen coursebooks specially designed for distance-learning will have been written, published and revised, with accompanying audio tapes, about forty-six video programmes will have been produced, and the course will have been delivered on a trial basis to one thousand two hundred teachers in three yearly cohorts of four hundred.

Background to the project

Education in China

The population of China is over 1.2 billion. In 1995, when this project started, there were:

- 180,438 kindergartens with 27,110,000 students
- 668,685 primary schools with 131,950,000 students
- 67,029 junior middle schools with 46,578,200 students
- 13,991 senior middle schools with 7,131,600 students
- 1,379 special schools with 295,600 students

The total number of teachers in 1995 was:

- 5,735,800 in primary schools
- 4,156,600 in secondary schools

The estimate for the number of secondary school teachers of English lacking the required BA degree in 1995 was 300,000. That is the target population to benefit from this project.

Table 1 Chinese school years

	Age	
Primary	6-7	
school	7	
	8	9 years of
	9	compulsory
	10	basic
	11	education
Junior middle	12	
school	13	
	14	
Senior middle	15	
school	16	
	17	

Changing situation in China

* With the advent of the Open Door Policy in China came an influx of foreign investment and an increase in foreign trade encouraged by the Chinese government. Joint ventures and fully owned foreign companies started to establish themselves, particularly along the eastern seaboard, so cities like Shanghai and Guangzhou saw rapid development. The government also set up Special Economic Zones, like Shenzhen and Zhuhai, to encourage foreign investors and to promote the establishment of factories and trade outlets. This economic development had a profound impact on China's social and education policy.

* It became clear to the Chinese that there was a strong link between their ability to use foreign languages, English in particular, and their ability to develop economically and create closer contacts with the outside world. It was accepted that the initial training they needed to catch up with world developments would come from outside. The government agreed to allow large numbers of foreign experts into the country to provide such training, but this could not be managed without a language for the two sides to communicate in.

* The Chinese government saw the importance of English to their nation's development, and so the SEdC made attempts to promote the teaching of it in secondary schools and to improve the teaching methods used.

- Amongst the professional community of China there has been an enormous increase in computer literacy: computer contacts made by means of the Internet and e-mail have had a significant impact on professional activity in China. It is usual these days for Chinese economists, international legal experts, and academics in all fields to have close links with their fellow professionals abroad. This, again, can only be achieved by means of a certain proficiency in a foreign language, and mostly in English.

- The opportunities for those who are proficient in English for employment in the better paid jobs and for obtaining scholarships to study and train abroad are far greater than for those without English or another foreign language. The demand for English learning is thus increasing all the time.

- The negative effect of the rapid economic development is the creation of a gulf between the richer, more developed eastern coastal areas and the poorer, less developed, western rural areas. Much of the north and west of the country is suffering from the closure of large-scale but economically non-viable state industries, creating mass unemployment of about twenty-seven per cent overall. The government is aware of this problem and is putting a certain amount of effort into educating and retraining those in the rural and old industrial areas. Distance education is a viable option in dealing with this problem.

Change in methodology

When China was closed, English was taught as an intellectual discipline. No need was seen to communicate in the language on a daily basis. The Chinese had developed their own version of the Grammar Translation Method. Teaching English was totally based on textbooks, and the basis of textbooks were texts usually with Chinese themes written in English by Chinese professors, with a heavy concentration on reading, translation and learning grammar and vocabulary.

As mentioned in the previous section, the opening up of China created new trade opportunities and the new foreign and joint ventures provided a wider range of employment opportunities for Chinese people with proficiency in English. There were suddenly many more training possibilities abroad through the medium of English and the need was created for communication skills in English. The whole emphasis in learning the language changed.

An SEdC project was started at the beginning of the 1990s to rewrite the middle school textbooks. UK consultants were commissioned with Chinese ELT specialists to design textbooks based on a more communicative approach. They are now used in most schools in China. And so, due to the policy of the SEdC, the emphasis in teaching the language has also changed. The textbook still has a specified structural syllabus, but 'communicative functions' have now been added, and all four language skills are to be trained, with much greater emphasis on the oral skills. The SEdC also brought in a new policy that required all senior middle school teachers to have a full BA degree in their subject, instead of the previously acceptable two year diploma. This would mean the up-grading of teachers' qualifications on a massive scale around the country.

Effect of change: problems of innovation

- With the introduction of new textbooks based on new teaching methods, the teachers require training and support in order to adapt their teaching from the old methods to the new.

- Another problem is that the state examination system and in particular the all-powerful college entrance examination has not changed. Students are still tested in the traditional way on their 'mastery' of the items in the structural syllabus, and their oral skills are not examined. The washback effect of this is not favourable towards the adoption of communicative teaching.

- Some teachers are still using the old methods with the new books. The effect of this is that there is no change for the students, and they fail to benefit from the changes introduced.

- This point is common to teachers in many countries where access to English-speaking cultures is difficult and the teachers' own competence in the language and culture is limited. Many teachers in China find the communicative approach threatening. With their lack of confidence in their own competence in English, they feel stressed by the alien cultural bias of the texts, frightened of students' questions which might expose their ignorance, and worried by what they see as their lack of control in the communicative activities. They prefer the security of texts about familiar topics, and having total control of the class, which means they ask all the questions and nominate students to answer, with everything taught well prepared in advance and nothing unexpected likely to happen. The previous textbooks and methodology provided such security.

- As most middle school teachers graduated from a two year diploma course, their own proficiency in English is limited. They feel unable to communicate in the language themselves, so feel unable to teach students to communicate in it.

- One cannot deny the importance of the Confucian influence on education in China. The teacher is still seen as the main source of knowledge. Students are thought of as empty vessels waiting to be filled. In order to show respect to the authority of the teacher, students should remain silent until they are told to speak. Classes are dominated by the teacher. Thus one finds unfavourable conditions for communicative methodology in the Chinese education system. Even when English teachers are willing to teach communicatively, there may still be much negative influence from the teachers of other disciplines in the school, and from the school head. In one case, a young English teacher in Shanghai was criticised by the maths teacher who taught the same group after her lesson, as whenever he set the students mathematical problems to solve, they tried to work with each other! He had come to observe her class and immediately understood the cause of the trouble, when he saw the students working in pairs and groups for much of the lesson.

The project
Origin of the project

- BFSU had been training middle school teachers for several years with the benefit of ODA-sponsored projects, upgrading their initial two year diploma to a full BA degree by means of a two year residential course at the university. The School of English Communication Studies at BFSU proposed to convert the materials developed in that project into nation-wide distance learning courses in book form. This would provide the necessary in-service training to a larger number of teachers around the country as well as providing publishing and research facilities for the group (of about ten or so) well trained teachers who had been involved in that project.

- The two year residential course in Beijing was proving problematic as it was no longer cost-effective for the university. Universities in China are under great pressure to increase their revenue and become self-funding. The potential customers for this course, the provincial schools, were becoming less willing to release their teachers for training, due to the shortage of teachers of English, and the expense of paying their salary plus the cost of the course. With lack of funding from their local education authorities, the difficulties for the provincial teachers to travel to Beijing and live there for two years would be insurmountable in most cases. The local authorities were also becoming aware that many teachers ended up settling in Beijing and did not return, leading to a loss of their investment. The university has now decided to stop running this course.

- The conditions were becoming more favourable for running the course by distance. This would involve far less expense on the part of the local authorities and would not aggravate the problem of the shortage of teachers.

- Thus, a new situation presented itself and the emphasis of the proposed project changed. BFSU, the SEdC and the ODA, and finally the CCRTVU became involved in devising a new plan for creating a distance-learning BA degree, lasting three years, to upgrade the teaching qualifications of the middle school teachers. It was decided that BFSU would create coursebooks specially designed for the distance degree course and that CCRTVU, with its vast network of radio and television universities around the country, would be permitted to administer the course and award the degree, under the auspices of the SEdC and with specialist help provided by the ODA.

CCRTVU network

The CCRTVU is an institution of higher education directly under the State Education Commission. It runs multimedia distance higher education courses using radio, television, print, and audio-visual teaching materials. The central university is in Beijing, and organises courses and examinations for 44 provincial Radio and Television Universities (RTVUs). Dependent on these are 831 branch schools at prefecture and city level, and 1699 work stations at county level; altogether more than 10,000 teaching classes that cover China's rural and urban areas. At any one time there are around a million students in the system, of whom 700,000 are degree students.

Tertiary education in China falls into two broad categories, one of which offers mainly four year degree courses (Daben) while the other provides two or three year practical courses (Dazhuan). The CCRTVU used to offer only Dazhuan courses for adult education. The decision by the SEdC (now Ministry of Education) to authorise the new distance BA as a Daben level degree from CCRTVU was therefore a most significant promotion for the institution, a deliberate move by the Ministry of Education to upgrade the CCRTVU system as a whole.

CCRTVU RESPONSIBILITIES IN THE PROJECT
CCRTVU is responsible for the following:
* entry examination and registration of students for the course at provincial level (NB the long-term aim is for the degree to be open to any middle school teacher, but for the pilot period it was decided to screen initial applicants to ensure high standards);
* delivery and transmission of all course materials;
* day-to-day administration of all courses;
* production of video support materials for the courses;
* administration of tutorial support;
* selection and training of course tutors;
* administration of all examinations;
* final certification for graduate students.

DIFFERENCE BETWEEN CCRTVU AND OTHER OPEN AND DISTANCE EDUCATION SYSTEMS
The CCRTVU system is the largest university in the world with its million students – the leader in size of all the mega-universities. Because of its use of the media, particularly television, in the dissemination of courses and materials from a centralised source, it comes within the definition of open and distance education, and indeed is often referred to as the Chinese Open University in lay discussion. However, the CCRTVU system differs in a major way from most other distance operations at tertiary level in that where the standard distance course transmits materials to students studying as individuals at home (or sometimes in the workplace) without classmates or a teacher, the CCRTVU system transmits courses to other campuses where part- or full-time students are studying as a class with a teacher.

EFFECTS OF THIS DIFFERENCE
Need to train lecturers to be tutors   Because the CCRTVU is essentially a campus system, it is not surprising that the typical television university lecturer teaches in the traditional campus way: one hour lectures supported by notes on the blackboard delivered to a class who take down the notes largely in silence with little or no two-way interaction between teacher and learner. The use of television scarcely changes this methodology: most programmes are 'talking head' – or even 'talking blackboard' – lectures with, naturally, even less interaction between lecturer and student.

With the new distance degree, however, a different kind of 'teacher' is required. There are no lectures, because there are no classes; students work at home in the evenings and at weekends. But there are tutorials, the normal provision being one two-hour session per week. These tutorials are there for the students to interact with each other and the tutor. They are there for discussion, debate, problem-solving and experience-sharing. Given that the student has to get through a minimum of ten hours' private study a week with the textbook, the tutor clearly cannot – and should not – teach the book. What, therefore should the tutor do, and where could she learn the skills and techniques required? CCRTVU's responsibility was to train lecturers appropriately.

Failure of the CCRTVU fully to exploit the advantages of open and distance education   If we take the Open University of the UK (UKOU) as a model for the standard open and distance educational system, we can see the following beneficial outcomes:
- a system of educational provision that is flexible and learner-centred through its openness and use of distance technology;
- an educational institution that has a radical influence towards change in general educational philosophy and practice;
- a 'second chance' provision that avoids being 'second rate';
- a system that allows for great economies of scale, for example in the production of textbooks, where standard OU books are used by all other universities, and in staff-students ratios, where 815 full-time OU staff provide courses for 200,000 students;
- a system that achieves all these things with the added advantage of much lower per student cost to the community (typically between forty and fifty per cent of the cost of traditional campus education).

The only one of the above outcomes shared by the CCRTVU system is the cost-effectiveness, which averages fifty per cent like the UKOU. This naturally makes it popular with the authorities, but unlike the OU, the CCRTVU system can scarcely claim to lead educational practice in China. What it is, its critics claim, is a second – or even third – rank of university provision that works in exactly the same way as other universities, but accepts a lower standard of student. In other words, it is second-chance and second-best, and it suffers from this judgement because it is neither truly open nor truly distance, as described above.

The new distance BA in TEFL, if successful, could be the forerunner of and the model for a truly open and distance system, one which could revolutionise educational provision in China. In terms of staff-student ratios, for example, with twenty-five times the staff of the OU, the CCRTVU system only teaches five times the students. Clearly there is the capacity to multiply student numbers significantly inside a very short period of time. This is the belief of those involved in the project, and is seen as a possibility by the Ministry of Education which authorises it.

THE TUTOR TRAINING COURSE

Initial research In order to design a sympathetic training course that would achieve practical results, we started with a questionnaire to all students and tutors and fact-finding visits to five of the six centres running the first year of the programme. Our basic findings were that:

- students' main problem was one of time and their personal management of it;
- tutors and students had not fully recognised how different distance study is to all they had ever done in education;
- tutors and students had difficulty recognising the different characteristics of a distance textbook;
- they had little understanding of a skills-based examination rather than a memory test;
- tutors and students found it difficult to distinguish between the roles of lecturer or teacher and the different role of tutor;
- conversely, they were still uncertain of the role of the learner, particularly in relation to the need for the learner to be self-motivated rather than teacher-directed;
- tutors needed assistance and training in the areas of tutorial planning and classroom organisation/management;
- they also needed an introduction to the theoretical and methodological background of the new textbooks;
- they needed a thorough discussion of all the implications of distance and open learning;
- they needed and wanted training in interpersonal communication skills.

Course design Our course was designed to fulfil the needs and solve the problems noted above. For it we produced:

- Timetable and syllabus; 10 pages
- Handouts with task-completion exercises; 28 pages
- Training videos: (average 30 mins. each)
    Open and Distance Learning
    Theoretical Background
    The Coursebooks
    The Learner
    The Tutor

The training videos took the title of each of the first five days of the seminar and explored the topic through interviews with experts, students, and tutors. The handout material was task-based, designed for individual and group discovery procedures, and when the fill-in tasks were completed they provided a record of the entire seminar. For the sixth day, participants in groups presented a summary of one of the major topics through any medium they chose: lecture, role play, drama, song.

Course procedure: the open secret Although it was nowhere stated in the materials or the syllabus, the course was organised along the learner-centred, communicative, task-based lines of a good tutorial, using the standard techniques of modern western seminar/workshops (which are still relatively new in China). That the seminar itself was an example of a good tutorial was therefore an open secret which the participants were supposed to uncover themselves, and on average they did this successfully by about the third day.

Results   Two major training seminars were held at which a total of one hundred CCRTVU lecturers from twenty-four out of the thirty-five provinces of China were trained. A feedback questionnaire to participants at the end revealed an overall rating score of 8.6 out of 10 for the course, putting it in the 'excellent' category.

Materials writing   The writing team consists of about ten counterparts, nearly all of whom have been sent to the UK on MA courses. It should be mentioned that none of these teachers are given time off their full teaching load to write these materials, which provides a constant race against the clock. The ODA provided funds for UK consultants on developing distance materials in the first years of the project. Training seminars were given to the team in writing distance materials. A three year syllabus for the BA degree in TEFL was designed in collaboration with the English Department of CCRTVU and was approved by the SEdC:

Year 1: focuses on basic language improvement and culture
The methodology on which the courses are based takes a communicative approach, giving the students plenty of practice in what they will later study in the methodology modules in Year 3.
Year 2: focuses on deeper study into the language and culture
Year 3: focuses on ELT methodology and professional development
The writers refer to the new school textbooks as much as possible, with many texts and tasks taken from them and exploited further for the training of language skills. In the final module, Practical Project Design, the students are required to plan their own classroom-based research project.

The actual writing is done in teams. Once the syllabus was agreed and approved by the authorities, the individual course modules were split into units, and individual writers were identified for each unit. The UK-appointed ELT specialist co-ordinates the whole process by holding regular project meetings, and providing training, consultancy and writing when required. The ELT specialist then co-ordinates an entire coursebook, providing the continuity and correcting the final writing. The Dean of the School of English Language Communication at BFSU, the overall co-ordinator of the writing of the coursebooks, then does the final editing.

The written materials are then sent to the university publishing house, one of the biggest educational publishers in the country, in camera-ready form. The publisher then only has to add the specified illustrations and print and bind the coursebooks. The audio cassettes that accompany the written materials are recorded by native-speaker teachers and a few Chinese teachers in the university press recording studio. The books and cassettes are published in a period of four to six weeks and are distributed to the regional RTVU centres in time for the next semester's course. The materials used for the first three years are trial versions, and need to be corrected, re-edited and where necessary rewritten.

FOCUS ON SPECIFIC PROBLEMS IN THE MATERIALS WRITING

Learner profile   From the data gained from questionnaires given at the beginning of the course and interviews with random students during the course, a learner profile was identified. Our average learner is a female teacher of between thirty and thirty-five years of age, with one young child, teaching a full timetable and with little time to study. Different learners organise their learning time differently. Some study in blocks of two to three hours at set times during the week, for example, and others literally grab an hour or so when they can get it. We assume that they have little support in their attempt to study and little help with their household duties. However, this cannot necessarily affect our writing. What does affect our writing is our assumption that the learner lacks confidence and needs constant support and encouragement. This is given in the wording of our tasks and instructions and in the feedback to the tasks.

Creating manageable chunks for self-study   The material is designed in such a way that it consists of reasonably self-contained chunks of material to work through, as we realise that our learners may not all have long periods of study time. Each Unit is divided into Activities and each Activity is divided into Tasks. Each Task then has Feedback provided.

Using discovery techniques instead of lecture   This is something that the writing team found difficult and they have developed a number of different ways of coping with it. One has written pre-reading questions on a piece of narrative text and then given feedback at the end. In 'Focus on Speaking', the writer includes descriptions of lessons all teaching the same function, but presenting it in different ways. The student is asked questions on the different approaches in order to compare and evaluate them. A similar technique is used in 'Focus on Grammar' for teaching the deductive and inductive approaches, except these were in the form of simplified lesson transcripts also accompanied by questions asking the student to compare and evaluate the two approaches. The whole approach in the methodology modules was to encourage the student to evaluate different aspects of teaching for herself and to try out new techniques and strategies whenever possible in her own lessons.

Giving feedback   Before writing the feedback the writers were asked to imagine the student sitting there beside them and to treat it like a one-to-one tutorial with a kind encouraging tone, trying to boost morale as much as possible. In 'Focus on Reading', the student is asked to design her own while-reading activities on a given text and then is given in the feedback three possible activities that the writer herself has designed, preceded by the comment: 'Now compare your activities with the ones below and see which ones you prefer'. Sometimes, the writer predicts what the student will answer to a question and conducts an imaginary discussion.

Video production

LANGUAGE AND CULTURAL SUPPORT VIDEOS: ASSUMPTIONS

In our initial planning we made the following assumptions concerning the language and culture support videos:

- the videos would provide language and cultural support to the coursebooks, and would follow their titles and topics but without any direct reference to or from the text, partly because the coursebooks had already been written without making any reference to videos, but also because it was considered that stand-alone videos had other advantages both educationally and commercially;

- the videos would feature authentic native-speaker English as far as possible, since they might be the only chance of such exposure for many teachers;

- international second-language varieties of English would also be exemplified because of their importance in the Chinese situation – English being the lingua franca of joint-venture companies, for example: there would be inter- active tasks connected with the basic text to motivate the students and focus their concentration; there would be no budget for copyright fees or extensive location recording, a financial restriction we share with the textbook writing team.

Format   The video series follows the user-friendly format of the coursebook distance materials, including:
- introduction of performance objectives;
- identification of language and study skills to be practised;
- pre-questions concerning the basic text for focus;
- a variety of text types, e.g. unscripted interviews with real people recorded by CCRTVU staff in Britain and China; scripted documentaries with voiceover; real-life role play (e.g. a mock-up of an interview arranged by staff of Nokia); copyright-free feature videos from British, American and Australian Embassy information offices.
- exercise tasks plus repeats of sections of text dealt with in the task;
- summary of objectives.

METHODOLOGY VIDEOS: ASSUMPTIONS

Unlike the language and culture videos, the methodology videos are being developed at the same time as the coursebooks and the following decisions were made in the planning stage:
- the series could be more integrated with coursebooks, with cross-references as appropriate, since the videos would not have the same general potential as the language and culture series;
- we would try to video real as opposed to rehearsed lessons, with teachers who employed communicative teaching in their classes;
- since such teachers are relatively rare in China, it was accepted that the teachers selected would be model teachers from key schools;

- identification of the teachers was to be made through the Ministry Inspectorate;
- writing team members would work with teachers on the lesson plan to ensure that all relevant points were covered, but the lesson would be essentially the teacher's own lesson following the textbook unit for that week.

Format   There are six 25-minute videos focusing on:
Reading
Listening
Talking
Lesson Planning
Classroom Management
Oral Interview Techniques.

- Each video starts with a summary of its objectives.
- There is a brief interview with the teacher before her lesson.
- This is followed by an edited version of the lesson (forty-five minutes edited down to approximately fifteen minutes).
- There is a brief teacher reflection after she has viewed her lesson.
- There is a limited commentary by the writer for that topic from the writing team.
- The video finishes with a summary of its objectives.

On-going evaluation and feedback

In order to obtain as much information as possible about the mistakes in the books and the problems and difficulties in studying caused by them, detailed questionnaires in Chinese from BFSU are distributed with each book. When these are completed by the students, they are returned to the local tutors, sent to the centre at CCRTVU and then passed on to BFSU for data processing. The students are asked to give feedback on the course module content, the nature of the tasks and the layout of the materials. We plan to visit each of the main tutorial centres around the country and collect more detailed feedback from individual students and their tutors. We will then have to collate this information and take decisions on the corrections that are to be made.The materials will be revised and rewritten.

Impact

We have yet to investigate the full impact of the project. We would like to investigate:
- the effect of the course on the proficiency of English of the teachers taking the course and of their students, especially in the rural areas of China;
- the opportunities, if any, afforded to the teachers because of their taking the course, such as promotion in their work, further training, research, or awards;
- the value of the specially designed distance materials and their effectiveness in helping the teachers manage their study in a self-sufficient way.

Outcomes

Various expected and unexpected products have come out of this project so far, which may have significance for future education, and in particular distance education, projects in China:

- BFSU has developed a well trained and experienced team of distance-learning writers, who can now offer future consultancy and training if required. If distance education materials are to be written in other subject areas in China, the skills of this team could be invaluable.

- CCRTVU has developed a well trained and experienced team of video-makers for distance-learning courses, which has importance for broadcasting opportunities in the future if further distance-learning courses are to be designed.

- One of the reasons for the success of this project was the collaboration between the two Chinese universities. This is as unusual in China as it is elsewhere. Because both universities had their separate and non-competing roles and both were dependent upon the success of the other, it was in their interests to maintain friendly and successful co-operation.

- A series of materials has been developed for self-study, which can serve as a model for future distance or self-study courses.

Conclusion

This is the first truly open distance-learning degree in China and provides lessons to be learnt for others attempting to set up similar degree courses. There is now a popular movement towards distance courses in China, but little research has gone into the designing of special materials or the training of the students in study strategies. There are training possibilities for other courses and other universities both in the development of materials and for using or reproducing the network that is already in place.

In particular we believe that the CCRTVU system will be energised to make a radical change in its overall degree provision. If the forty-four present campuses became centres for fully open and distance education, student numbers could be multiplied two or three times within a relatively short time span, solving much of the country's problem of tertiary educational provision.

This project is of great importance for DFID and the Chinese Ministry of Education, as it paves the way for future training courses to address the problems of poverty, unemployment and underdevelopment in parts of China, particularly the rural areas without access to the education or training facilities in the big cities.

5 Cultural Studies Syllabus and Materials: A Writing Partnership

Leah Davcheva
British Council, Sofia

Helen Reid-Thomas
University of Strathclyde, Glasgow

Alan Pulverness
Norwich Institute of Language Education

The syllabus project

This paper will report on the Cultural Syllabus and Materials Design Project run by the British Council in Bulgaria during the late 1990s. Now that the writing project is complete and the syllabus is ready for use in English and other foreign language classrooms, it is important to reflect critically on the overall nature of the writing process and to demonstrate that the two key ideas which have been driving it forward have been innovation and partnership.

The first part of this paper will attempt to answer the following questions:
- Who wrote the syllabus?
- How and why?
- Who is the syllabus for? Who will use it?
- What is innovative about the syllabus and the writing process itself?
- How does partnership come into the picture?

Who wrote the syllabus?

The cultural studies syllabus was written by a group of sixty teachers of English. They all belong to a cultural studies network set up in 1993. They are, in the majority, secondary school teachers of English. Among them are teachers from the higher education sector and also British teachers of English teaching in English-medium schools in Bulgaria.

How and why?

The writing of the syllabus took place during writing seminars, of which there were six for the whole project. Two syllabus consultants facilitated and guided the steps of the writing process. After the completion of each writing seminar, there was a period for trialling the new teaching materials that had been produced and for carrying out various writing and evaluation tasks. There is not just one single, correct answer to the question why the teachers set themselves this enormous task. The reasons are both historical and logical. Let's go back to the setting up of the network. From the very beginning of its existence it had a number of goals, but its prior aim was to train the teachers in new approaches to the teaching and study of culture in English language classrooms.

As well as working towards the achievement of its main goal, the network provided mechanisms for the sharing of ideas among the networking teachers. There were concerted efforts at recording the initial steps in the process of cultural teaching and learning. By the time the teachers started their work on the syllabus they had been through important stages in the production of various types of materials. Chronologically the tool that was first devised was the diary sheet. This was a specially designed lesson record form which the teachers used to evaluate their own cultural studies lessons in terms of lesson objectives and topics, materials, teacher-student interaction and degree of success. Produced by individual teachers for sharing within the network, the diary sheets had a limited circulation. They reached other English teaching colleagues, but their main role was to promote the exchange of ideas and materials within the network.

The next tool that was designed to ensure the sharing of experience was the network's newsletter. Schools on the network have taken turns to produce NetNews and several issues have come out. One of the early objectives of the newsletter was to encourage more and more members of the network to express themselves in writing. Very soon, however, the bulletin added on the role of representing the network to a growing group of 'outsiders': school colleagues and the wider ELT community. NetNews is aimed at making the network known and respected for the innovative work the teachers are doing. It is a manifestation of the teachers' pride and satisfaction that they themselves are making it possible for their publication to come out, thus carving out a special kind of space for themselves.

The first truly collective production effort of the networking teachers was the series of five materials packages, each on a separate topic. During the planning stage the teachers gave three reasons why they thought the packages would be the most logical and justifiable direction that the activities of the network should take. The most important reason was the lack of suitable ready-made materials which they could successfully use to facilitate cultural learning in their English lessons. The teachers felt that commercially produced materials, however professional and good they could be, lacked the Bulgarian cultural perspective and the unique classroom insights of the teachers who were getting quite confident in what they thought their students needed in terms of intercultural education. The second reason was the willingness of the teachers to move from a reception to a production stage in their training and development process. The time had come for them to make that decisive step towards putting into practice some of the most useful ideas inspired by their training. The third motive driving them towards the production of something 'tangible and usable' was the desire to start building up an image of the network as a large group of teachers whose training and work had the potential of benefiting not only themselves, but their schools, their students and the whole English language teaching community in the country. The culmination of the teachers' urge to spread their ideas and what they saw as innovative teaching practice was the writing of the syllabus. The syllabus project was an initiative which was structured and organised in such a way as to produce maximum impact on the practice of language and culture learning in Bulgaria. Through writing the syllabus and later by training other teachers to use it, the networking teachers aim to encourage their colleagues to change their perceptions and approaches to teaching so that the boundaries of FLT could be redefined in accordance with the new political, social and European context.

Cultural teaching, as information-giving and the endless provision of facts, has always been fairly popular as the bedrock of the Bulgarian attitude to education is the craving for knowledge, for more and more facts. What has been missing, though, is the need to find out the connection between these facts, the need to teach towards the critical understanding of the learners' own society and the societies of the people whose language they are learning.

Who is the syllabus for?

The syllabus targets several groups of users:
* teachers of English in English-medium schools
* teachers of English in comprehensive schools
* teacher trainers, pre-/in-service
* student teachers of English
* teachers of history, geography, Bulgarian language and literature, and of other foreign languages
* school heads
* publishers
* educationalists.

The networking teachers have themselves suggested ways for the syllabus ideas to reach as wide an audience as possible. This will happen through:
* seminars for teachers and also head teachers
* cultural studies summer schools
* cultural studies day (together with IATEFL – International Association of Teachers of English as a Foreign Language)
* culture learning noticeboards
* lesson observation
* general staff meetings in schools
* involvement of native-speaker teachers and teacher trainers
* teacher development hours
* informal conversations
* NetNews and other publicity
* students as a factor to challenge teachers
* school visits
* team teaching
* 'come any time', but also specific invitation
* SOS – 'Can you help me?'
* conferences and other forums
* the Internet.

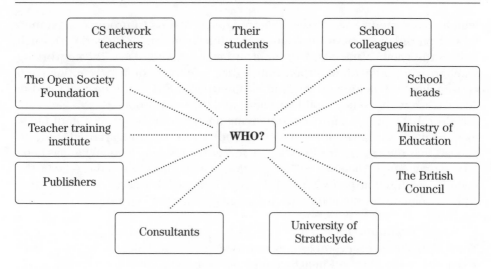

Figure 1   The partnership

Innovation and change

In view of the project's products and achievements, we regard the writing of the syllabus as a steady process of development which led to three significant outcomes. First and foremost the syllabus materialised as a quality publication and was formally acknowledged by the educational authorities. It filled a gap in the pedagogical space of the country. Unlike all other foreign language teaching programmes the syllabus is skills- rather than knowledge-led. It involves new culture learning methodology oriented towards critical reading, comparing and contrasting, ethnography and research. Secondly, the teachers who were involved in its creation experienced unprecedented professional growth and acquired new skills and classroom behaviour. They had the courage to trial the new ideas, to teach their way through the unknown and the novel. Thirdly, a number of new pedagogical values emerged, were voiced and consolidated through research, classroom practice and sharing.

Partnership

It became possible for the project innovations to spread thanks to the purposeful construction of relationships of trust and collaboration among the various participating parties. Figure 1 presents the idea of partnership which helped promote change and enabled newness to filter through the system.

The network's chief partner has always been the British Council. Its role has been to listen carefully to what the teachers say, to look at what they do and how they do it and to try and define the trends and directions of change. It responded to the teachers' wants by setting up and running the syllabus project. The Council provided strong leadership and ensured that there was good communication among the participants.

Another important partner of the network and important agent of change has been the Bulgarian Ministry of Education. Its role can best be described by the word empowerment. From the very start of the project the Ministry empowered the teachers to innovate, experiment, and go all the way to redefining their beliefs and values. Together with the Ministry of Education, the Central Teacher Training Institute also put its support and prestige behind the implementation of the syllabus ideas. As the diagram shows, the networking teachers also received encouragement and co-operation from their head teachers and their colleagues. With very few exceptions a climate of trust was established in the participating schools and the authors of the syllabus could get as much observation, supervision and feedback as they desired and found feasible.

The teachers' main source of inspiration were their students. The students' successes and failures, their interest in and attitude to the new approach were the chief measure against which their teachers judged how to proceed with each successive step in the construction of the syllabus.

The writing project received its closest academic, research and strategic guidance from its two external consultants, both from Britain. They had both worked for other Bulgarian projects before and were familiar with the foreign language teaching scene. The role of the two consultants was to plan and structure the writing sessions within the framework of the whole process, to facilitate the work during the sessions, challenge the creative powers of the teachers, and provide both criticism and praise.

By way of concluding the description of the rationale, history and context of the syllabus project we would like to compare it to a carrier wave; a carrier wave for change. It succeeded in picking change at point A, articulated it, drove it forward to point B, where it is going to sweep off again, for yet another take-off.

Key principles

We now focus on the key principles that informed our thinking as work on the syllabus developed with the sixty teachers over the series of six workshops that were held between the inception of this phase of the project and the actual publication of the syllabus two years later.

We should emphasise at this point that neither the teachers, project manager nor consultants had a clear idea beforehand of what the evolved syllabus would look like or how it would be structured. These decisions were arrived at gradually through discussion and trialling of ideas in workshops and later in classrooms and with colleagues. We did, however, share a basic underlying conviction about the nature of cultural studies which should be made clear at the outset.

In most discussions of British cultural studies in recent years we can trace three recurrent strands of debate:
1 the relation in cultural studies between information ('knowledge') and analysis (leading to 'understanding');
2 the significance of the term 'British' in British cultural studies;
3 the way(s) in which the term 'cultural studies' is understood.

The first of these was something we discussed at some length in our workshops on the syllabus. The notion of British Studies as information-based and Britain-specific was familiar to all the teachers; however, they had all done a fair amount of in-service training before starting on the syllabus project, which for some had taken the form of a UK course in British cultural studies, and this experience led them to question received ideas about information-based courses and the relationship between 'knowledge about' and 'understanding of' cultures (including their own). They came to the conclusion that they wanted the syllabus to give primary place to developing in their students the ability to use tools for *understanding* by means of questioning and analysis of the *information* supplied in various forms, for example by the media, tourist literature, medical leaflets and literary texts.

Secondly, we discussed the issue of 'Britishness'. We all agreed that, although our particular interest had developed out of an ELT context, we understood cultural studies primarily as a field of comparative studies, generally between the home culture/cultures and those of the target language. 'Britishness' was, so to speak, incidental to the large project of cultural comparison. We do not think, therefore, that this particular project can be depicted either theoretically or in practice as yet another institutionalised mechanism of linguistic and cultural imperialism – not least because both the project managers and the vast majority of the teachers themselves are Bulgarian nationals. And indeed in the end we decided to leave out the word 'British' in our final version of the syllabus document in order to emphasise the wider application of the Cultural Syllabus.

Finally, what is/are cultural studies (CS) and what should be the aims of any language-related curriculum or syllabus in CS? Byram's work offers a valuable model in the way he has applied the insights of the Birmingham Centre for Contemporary Cultural Studies to the present context of language teaching and learning in schools and universities. However, the one question we might have about his work is the apparent idealisation of cultural contact, the assumption that intercultural exchanges are almost of their nature benign and positive. This has not always been the case and one of the values of cultural studies must be that it offers ways of understanding and problematising such contacts. Montgomery (1998) suggests that any developed programme in CS will aim to:

- enrich learning of the language;
- alert students to cultural difference;
- introduce them to theories of culture;
- provide them with techniques for describing and analysing cultures and also for comparing them;
- provide them with techniques for negotiating the distance between their own culture and that of others;
- enable them to conceptualise the operation of power within culture;
- theorise and trace points of articulation between major cultural institutions e.g. literature – language – media.

Our engagement as a group with these three major concerns, i.e. the relationship between knowledge and understanding; the meaning of 'British' in the phrase 'British cultural studies'; and the nature of cultural studies as an intellectual discipline shaped the way the syllabus developed and in particular the framework around which it was organised.

So how does that framework operate? Having initially considered the possibility of constructing the syllabus around topics, we decided to shift from that to focus on skills as the organising principle. Eventually, after much discussion, we narrowed these down to four broad categories:
- critical reading
- comparing and contrasting
- ethnography
- research.

This is not intended to be an exhaustive list – teachers using the syllabus may well add to it from their own experience – but it provides guidelines for a developmental approach to the teaching of cultural studies skills.

Critical reading skills   These develop from the basic reading skills through interrogation of the text to more advanced skills such as recognition of register and style and include many of the usual reading skills which are then developed with a cultural studies focus.

Comparing and contrasting elements in C1 (the 'home' culture) and C2 (the 'target' culture) leading hopefully to attitudinal change towards that which is different and 'other'. In our table (see appendix) this macro skill, in conjunction with the ethnographic skills, is the means by which the affective element, which brings about those changes in attitude so crucial to cultural studies, is most clearly explored.

Ethnographic skills   This is perhaps the central concept in our understanding of cultural studies. Of course, we do not suggest that students can be turned into ethnographers in a couple of lessons but we do try to develop certain key ethnographic skills, namely the practice of participant observation and learning to ask certain kinds of questions of any text or cultural event or institution: in the materials there are sample lessons on e.g. the Bulgarian satirical TV programme *Kanaleto*; the birth of a baby, in Bulgaria and in Britain; Bulgarian and British tourist leaflets. These skills are developed initially in relation to the home culture, through local visits and projects, and than applied to the C2.

Research skills   As with critical reading skills, there is considerable overlap here with the skills learnt in any language classroom and indeed in any subject where project work is a focus: they include the collection of data by variety of means, the appreciation of the difference between qualitative and quantitative data, the use and acknowledgement of sources, (for a more comprehensive list of the skills involved see appendix).

The syllabus contains an introduction telling the story of the project and setting out the principles on which it is based. It also includes a set of teaching materials which were developed by the teachers in the workshops, then trialled and revised, and these offer exemplars of the various skills in action.

We decided the syllabus should be *skills* rather than *topics* based. This does not mean that topics have been altogether ignored and we spent considerable time on defining a set of broad topic areas which are developed and recycled through the classes from the preparatory to the final year. They include areas such as History and Heritage, the Media, Education, Family and Social Relations.

One further important consideration was making the links between the language coursebooks and the cultural studies syllabus. Because the situation at present is somewhat complicated by the fact that while in the more advanced classes the old books are still in use, two new coursebooks are available at the preparatory level, and some schools use one and some the other. What we have done is to indicate in the teaching materials where there is a direct link to a particular lesson and where there is a general link to a topic area treated in one or other of the coursebooks. We also emphasise the value of the 'cultural studies moment' in a language class (Kramsch, 1993) where a language question may give rise to a discussion of a cultural issue.

Key issues
Models of curriculum renewal

The project was an excellent demonstration of a genuinely progressivist form of curriculum renewal. This model is distinguished by Clark (1987) from the classical humanist approach (where change is formulated at university level and imposed through the education hierarchy) and the reconstructionist approach (where change is based on needs analysis and implemented through a cycle of 'Research, Development and Dissemination'). By contrast, ours was a wholly bottom-up initiative, generated by the teachers in the British Studies network, whose work had reached the point where they themselves decided on the need for a cultural studies syllabus.

Mutual trust

For the project to succeed, we depended upon a circle of trust among all the parties involved – i.e. the project manager, the consultants and the group of teachers writing the syllabus. We could not have enjoyed this reciprocal trust had it not been for the history of previous collaboration and the degree of shared awareness that it produced.

Exploratory process

It was difficult – though vital – for the group to accept that although the consultants were fully prepared to provide a range of options for syllabus design and content, there was no pre-existing template that was being coaxed into existence. The consultants' role was to enable the teachers to develop their syllabus.

Responsive planning

The exploratory nature of the process meant that at each state of the project, the frameworking provided by the consultants had to be as flexible and open as possible. Thus, although the overall timetable was determined by the project manager, the decisions made about the content and procedure of each separate stage were made largely in response to the directions taken by the teachers.

Involvement of whole group

Organisationally, perhaps the greatest challenge was to ensure a sense of ownership by involving the entire group of approximately sixty teachers. The nature of this involvement varied at different stages, with inventories of skills and topics produced by all sub-groups; early drafts of different sections of the syllabus documents written and redrafted by different groups; and specific editorial tasks allocated to individual groups in the later stages.

Role of native-speaker teachers

The project benefited from the involvement of several British teachers who were working in the English-medium schools. As well as acting as cultural and linguistic informants, they were able to contribute their own intercultural experience to complement that of their Bulgarian colleagues. The fact that they share the same working environment as many of the Bulgarian teachers focused their participation and their presence in the group was an extremely positive factor.

Design: flexibility – exemplification

A design problem that drove much of the group's work was the visualisation of the syllabus. Although the project involved a good deal of materials writing, we had to recognise that a syllabus is not a coursebook and if our syllabus was to be used, it had to be possible to combine it with a number of different language coursebooks. This constraint implied a syllabus which was sufficiently flexible to function as an integral part of different language programmes. The corollary is that the materials which formed part of the syllabus had to be regarded by users as exemplification and not as a kind of coursebook.

Terminology

A group of professionals working intensively on a project of this kind inevitably has recourse to a good deal of jargon (and generates some of its own!). Since we wanted the syllabus to be as user-friendly as possible, we decided to incorporate a comprehensive glossary, which included not only the specialist terminology which occured in the syllabus document itself, but also a range of key terms in the field of cultural studies. In this way we hoped to provide the basis for a discourse about cultural learning to develop amongst users of the syllabus, which went beyond the immediate application of the syllabus itself.

Ongoing evaluation (process and products)

Evaluation, both within the syllabus and of the syllabus, raises a number of important issues but perhaps the most crucial factor in evaluating the achievement of inter-cultural competence is the development of self-awareness in the learner in reflecting on, analysing and reacting to 'otherness' – the quality of the other culture.

Appendix: Skills for cultural studies

Critical reading	Comparing and contrasting	Ethnographic	Research
Basic reading skills Skim/scan reading Recognising sentence structure	Developing awareness of different starting points: C1>C1 C1>C2 C2>C2 C2>C1	Drawing on personal experience Observing people, places, behaviour, language Learning to be participant/observer in one's own culture Learning to be participant/observer in another culture	Asking questions Learning to use libraries and other resources Learning to record sources Learning to collect data selectively
Recognising typography and layout Recognising genre 'Interrogating' the text: asking WH – questioning to identify purpose, primary focus, target reader, author or originator of text and the way the message is conveyed Identifying sources	Developing C1/C2 comparisons: Identifying similarities and differences Recognising cultural misunderstanding Recognising and analysing culture specific attitudes and patterns of behaviour	Learning to ask the right kind of questions i.e. those which help the participant/observer to understand a cultural situation Finding the most useful sources of information	Responding to questionnaires Designing questionnaires Planning interviews Asking probing questions Making and taking notes Transcribing short extracts from interviews
Recognising stereotypes	Activating prior knowledge and experience, enabling students to make comparison and draw conclusions		
Recognising paragraph organisation Distinguishing between main and subordinate points			
Recognising types of modality Distinguishing between fact and opinion Responding to denotation/connotation Reading between the lines Recognising author's attitude/ emotion Recognising text structure	Recognising and developing sensitivity to difference Going beyond superficial similarity/difference Interpreting differences	Taking field notes Collecting, processing and analysing ethnographic data Differentiating between quantitative and qualitative data	Reading and interpreting statistical data: graphs, charts, etc.
Recognising style, register and mode(s) of address Recognising implied readership Recognising use of culturally distinctive stylistic devices (e.g. loaded adjectives, use of metaphor) 'Unpeeling' culturally loaded texts Deconstructing context of situation Drawing conclusions Avoiding over-generalisation	Achieving basic familiarity with one's own and other culture(s) Learning to be more detached about one's own culture and more tolerant of other cultures	Participating meaningfully in the context of one's culture and in the context of another culture Developing willingness to suspend judgement	Identifying research topic Designing a research project Planning and timing research Analysing and drawing conclusions from data Acknowledging sources Referencing

6 Teaching the Primary and Secondary Curriculum through the Medium of English

John Clegg
Educational Consultant, London

Introduction

I want to talk about teaching the primary and secondary curriculum through the medium of English. My shorthand for this is ESL. I want to argue that ESL is a distinct school of thought and practice within ELT and that it deserves a lot more attention than it gets. I also want to propose that the low profile it has in ELT is not good for ESL itself. I will be putting the case for ESL and suggesting how we might bring it into the ELT fold.

Schools of thought and practice

I am aware that EFL and ESL may mean different things to different people and I will start off by defining them for the purposes of this paper.

- By EFL, I mean English used for a fairly narrow range of societal functions, including, for example, tourism, entertainment and international communication.
- By ESL at primary and secondary level, I mean English used as a medium of instruction (MOI) in schools. So the main characteristic of school ESL is that it involves getting a school education through the medium of English as a second language. Usually, this occurs in contexts in which English also has a range of functions outside the school, including administration, politics, the law and the media; but not always.

The other boundaries which I will draw are between the three forms of ESL:

1 *Bilingual education* which refers specifically to the education of students in secondary schools through the medium of English as a second language. Here I will concentrate on European schools for the purposes of this paper (see also Brewster, this volume) though obviously bilingual education happens elsewhere.
2 *Minority education* (or EAL, which is what its practitioners in the UK now call it) which refers specifically to the mainstream education – i.e. the learning of curricular subject-matter knowledge and skills – of members of minority language communities.
3 *English-medium education* which refers specifically to the primary,

secondary (and tertiary) education of students in English-medium education systems overseas. I will focus here on African education systems (and exclusively on the primary and secondary sectors), but clearly there are others.

Before discussing these contexts separately, I will outline the chief characteristics of ESL which are common to all three.

Most of what happens in such contexts is not language teaching at all, as we know it, but the teaching and learning of the primary and secondary curriculum through English as a second language. It is true that in all three contexts, you are likely to find some English language being taught as a separate subject in the curriculum. But nevertheless, the majority of opportunities to use English communicatively occur outside the ESL classroom and in the mainstream curriculum. This situation compels us to adjust our view of what second-language learning is: it is certainly not something which only happens in the ESL classroom. We might also have to adjust our view of who language teachers are: whether they know it or not, mainstream primary classroom teachers and secondary subject teachers will probably be contributing more to the development of students' second-language ability than ESL specialists. A school which operates like this has enormous resources at its disposal for the teaching and learning of both language and curricular contents. You can improve language learning by harnessing the language development potential of mainstream subject teaching; and you can improve the learning of subject-matter knowledge by drawing attention to the central role of language within it. These are, of course, two sides of the same coin.

Not all schools which teach through a second language will take advantage of these possibilities. But what can encourage a school to do so is the recognition that, unless you do take seriously the role of language in learning, then getting educated through a second language is very difficult. It is difficult for students to learn school knowledge in a language in which they are still struggling. It is also difficult for teachers to teach, and they may be struggling with the language almost as much as their students. It is easy for the whole enterprise to fail and indeed it often does. There are plenty of students from ethnic minorities in the UK, for example, who leave school with qualifications well below those which they are capable of getting, thus adding to other disadvantages which they may have to face in an unequal society. And there are without doubt large proportions of the school populations in English-medium Africa, who fail to fulfil anything like their academic potential because it was simply too difficult – on top of other socioeconomic problems – to learn through a language they could not properly master.

However, some schools do collectively recognise that if you are operating through a second language, you can only provide a satisfactory education if you take language seriously. Schools which teach like this tend to take an approach to education which has typical characteristics. For example:

• There will normally be some form of separate, focused English teaching, but ideally it will be oriented to helping students learn strategies for using it as a tool for learning across the curriculum.

- Subject teachers will tend to be aware of the language demands which their subjects and their teaching style make on their students, and they will plan and teach with these language demands in mind, thus taking upon themselves some of the responsibility for the language of their area of the curriculum. Subject teachers may also work collaboratively with ESL teachers both in the planning and the execution of lessons (i.e. there will sometimes be two teachers in the classroom).

- The materials which subject teachers use will be produced, or even in rare cases published, with language demands in mind.

- The school will take collective decisions about how they manage the business of being more language-sensitive – of getting language across the curriculum, so to speak – and they will develop a whole-school policy on language issues.

So we can see that in this kind of school, ESL is a very stretched term. It stretches well beyond the boundaries of the ESL classroom proper and colonises English-medium subject classrooms – exploits them as much as possible for their language-learning value and contributes centrally to the learning of subjects. We can also see that the concepts of language teacher and subject teacher become fuzzy. Very often a language teacher might be teaching students language and how to use it to learn science; while the science teacher might be teaching them science and how to express it in language. What we are talking about here, is not so much language-learning, but education generally and the role of language within it.

However, it takes time and effort to get a school working in this way. A lot of English-medium schools do not manage it. In these cases, the typical picture is of students sitting in classrooms, engaged in an unequal struggle with both the subject-matter knowledge and the English language, and failing – perhaps miserably – to get themselves a proper education. In that sense English-medium teaching is a hazardous business; it is easy to get it wrong. I will be proposing later that it often does go wrong – especially in Africa, but also in minority education in the UK and less so in the successful highly literate middle-class context of European bilingual schooling.

To sum up, ESL in primary and secondary schools is a broad category: what counts as ESL ranges from language-focused lessons at one extreme, to language-sensitive content teaching at the other. It may be useful to posit two versions of ESL: one is a strong view, which characterises the collective effort of the school right across the curriculum, to ensure that the curriculum is taught with second-language development in mind. This version has a good chance of delivering an education. There is also a weak view of ESL, which refers solely to what goes on in English language classes and has little impact on content teaching, which in turn remains fairly inaccessible to students. This kind of schooling is an unreliable way of running a second-language-medium education system.

Schools of practice in ELT

The three schools of ESL practice will be described and evaluated in what follows. A brief comparison is shown in Table 1. EFL is dealt with briefly first, in order to set the ESL categories off against it.

EFL

SCHOOL ROLE/SOCIETAL FUNCTION OF ENGLISH
EFL operates in contexts in which English has a fairly narrow range of societal functions. A typical context might be France, Germany or the Netherlands. English occupies the 'foreign language' slot in the school curriculum.

EXPOSURE TO ENGLISH
Exposure to English is often not high, but it has high status as the language of choice for communication across political boundaries.

STATUS OF L1 OR COMMUNITY LANGUAGE
In these contexts, a local language is the MOI, has high status in the community and is not in danger of being displaced by English. We are talking, in other words, about an additive form of bilingualism.

MODEL OF PEDAGOGY
EFL has models of pedagogy which are fairly well defined: they are versions of communicative language teaching, with, for example, controlled input and practice, 'presentation, practice, production' forms of lesson shape, selection and grading of language items and a wide standard repertoire of classroom tasks.

TRAINING OPPORTUNITIES AND GENERAL HEALTH
EFL training opportunities are widespread, and generally the health of EFL is good in the UK and overseas, if measured by, for instance, published materials, academic courses, training courses and English language courses.

Bilingual education

Let us move now to the ESL category and the first of the three contexts in which English as a second language is the medium of primary or secondary instruction: namely bilingual education.

By bilingual education, I am referring to schools which teach their curriculum, wholly or partly through the medium of English and for the purposes of this paper, I am talking mainly about Western and Eastern Europe. The movement towards doing this is well established in Eastern Europe and rapidly gaining strength right across Western Europe. The people who work in it sometimes call it CLIL or 'content and language integrated learning'. There are about one hundred secondary schools in Germany which do this in English and about another fifty which do it in French and the numbers are growing. There are some seven hundred streams in French lycees which do it. The Finns are extremely active in it, and there is a lot of interest in it in Austria, the Netherlands and Sweden (Frühauf et al., 1996). It is interesting enough for German publishers to publish materials for geography and history through

Table 1 Comparing schools of practice in ELT

	EFL	Bilingual Education/CLIL	ESL	
			Minority Education/EAL	English-medium Education
School role of English	FL: separate curricular subject	MOI: partial or full, mainly secondary	MOI	MOI from scratch or early-primary or secondary
Societal functions of English	Narrow range of societal functions	Narrow range of societal functions	All key societal functions	Broad range of societal functions
Exposure to English	Low (- medium)	Low (- medium)	High	Low – high
Status/strength of L1/community language	High	High; additive bilingualism	Low; subtractive bilingualism and danger of language loss	High; additive bilingualism but L1 literacy weak, early and later
Integration of ELT with curriculum	Low	High	EAL 'mainstreamed', but resistance from subject-teachers	Low: ELT a separate subject; cross-curricular resistance to language
Model of pedagogy	Versions of CLT	Mix of language and subject-teaching processes	EAL pedagogy driven by demands of mainstream subjects	ELT: CLT developing; little integration with subjects
Training opportunities	Good	Scarce	Formerly good, but increasingly scarce	A lot of capacity, but not orientated to English-medium work
'Health' of this form of ELT	Good	Good start	Shaky: under-resourced; achievements unrecognised	ELT: struggling; cross curricular orientation/ influence low

CLIL Content and language integrated learning
EAL English as an additional language
EFL English as a foreign language
ESL English as a second language
MOI Medium of instruction

English as a second language, and for German universities to train teachers to teach through English. You can join the EU-funded EuroCLIC website (http://www.euroclic.net) and learn about it. The EU is specifically interested in this movement and mentions it (under the EU-speak heading of 'plurilingual education') in documents setting out the principles of educational development in Europe and in funding opportunities. Proponents of it are enthusiastic and see it not only as a way of getting a secondary education on an equal footing with L1-medium schooling, but as a means of learning a foreign language which will, they think, become the method of choice for doing this in the EU.

So what are the chief characteristics of bilingual education?

SCHOOL ROLE/SOCIETAL FUNCTION OF ENGLISH/EXPOSURE TO ENGLISH
It is interesting that it is happening in countries where English has a narrow range of societal functions, where exposure to English is low-middling; in other words, a typically EFL context. One might with some justification refer to it as a form of foreign language learning and indeed its most active proponents are foreign language teachers.

STATUS OF L1 OR COMMUNITY LANGUAGE
It is happening in countries where the official medium of instruction has high status. This is, again, an additive form of bilingualism.

INTEGRATION WITH CURRICULUM
It is a form of schooling which integrates as fully as possible second-language learning with the acquisition of subject-matter knowledge. In this sense, it is not really second-language learning. It is the learning of subject-matter knowledge through a second language. So it is centrally oriented to the role of language in learning. This characteristic is important; it applies to all the forms of ESL I am dealing with.

MODEL OF PEDAGOGY
People in bilingual education are still working out what kind of pedagogy they should use. However, it is not obviously indebted to concepts of syllabus design, controlled input and practice, selection and grading, and 'PPP'. It is much more closely linked to the processes which underlie the acquisition of subject-matter knowledge.

TRAINING OPPORTUNITIES
Training opportunities are few and far between, but some exist in Germany, for example initial teacher training at the University of Wuppertal.

STATE OF HEALTH
What about the general state of health of bilingual education? The answer is extremely vigorous and promising great things, if only measured in terms of EU support, internet activity perhaps, speed of developments, and the enthusiasm of its proponents. It is one of a growing number of areas of ELT, as highlighted by Graddol (1997), where the experts will be non-native speakers.

ESL in minority education/EAL

I will now turn to the second of my three categories of ESL: ESL in minority education or EAL. I will be referring primarily to the UK situation.

SCHOOL ROLE/SOCIETAL FUNCTION OF ENGLISH

By EAL, I mean the mainstream education of ethnolinguistic minorities in countries where English is the MOI and fulfils almost all the key societal functions, as for example in the UK. Go into any school in a metropolitan area of the UK and this is the educational experience of a significant minority – and in some schools the large majority – of pupils.

EXPOSURE TO ENGLISH/STATUS OF L1 OR COMMUNITY LANGUAGE

Exposure to English is high, but the status of minority languages tends to be low and there is a clear danger of them being displaced by English; in other words this is subtractive bilingualism in practice, and it is indeed often a publicly-stated goal of minority education. In contrast to bilingual education in Europe, authorities in the UK do not set out to maintain the first or community languages of these students and thus to encourage bilingualism.

INTEGRATION WITH CURRICULUM

As far as language/content integration is concerned, it is the policy of most UK Local Education Authorities (LEAs) to integrate the learning of EAL as far as possible with the learning of mainstream subjects. EAL students join mainstream classrooms as soon as possible on entry to a school. EAL teachers work collaboratively in mainstream classrooms with mainstream teachers, supporting EAL learners. In reality good 'partnerships' are rare and mainstream teachers – especially subject teachers in secondary schools – are somewhat resistant to the idea of teaching their subject in a way which is inclusive of and accessible to those students who are still struggling with English. Both EAL students and EAL teachers here have a status problem, a visibility problem. This contrasts strongly with the case of the secondary bilingual classroom in, say, Germany, where subject teachers are compelled by the logic of their classes of exclusively L2-learners to take account of the need to integrate language and content.

Nevertheless, the official model of British EAL is one in which English is supposed to be very much integrated with subject content. This is also, then, subject learning through the medium of English as a second language, as much as it is a form of ELT.

MODEL OF PEDAGOGY

EAL in the UK operates a model of pedagogy which I find fascinating. At its best (and I have indicated that this can be rare), it can be fully integrated with the teaching of curricular content. This is fascinating for linguists, who are looking to add meat to the content of ELT; and to subject teachers interested in the role of language in school learning.

TRAINING OPPORTUNITIES

Training opportunities for UK EAL teachers were once good. The providers of EAL training have mainly been the LEAs and specifically their language services and it is here that most of the expertise in EAL can be found. There was, until its demise in about 1992 due to insufficient funding, a highly successful national scheme of EAL training, leading to the RSA Diploma in Teaching English across the Curriculum in Multilingual Schools. In addition there has been some UK government-funded training of mainstream teachers, to take account of the range of ability in the MOI within their classrooms. But because EAL learners are not formally recognised in the national curriculum proper and have no legal entitlement to special forms of educational provision, and because funding follows entitlement, the prospect for EAL training in the immediate future is dismal.

STATE OF HEALTH

British EAL is not in a good state of health. Its achievements at the LEA and school level are good, and it has a small but active professional association. In the past it has been reasonably well funded directly from government through what is known as 'Section 11'. But funding has been cut back repeatedly. EAL still struggles for recognition on the margin of school life and of national educational provision.

Both the EFL and EAL branches of ELT have tended to avoid each other. EAL shares ideas easily with the movement for mother-tongue development and fairly well with the teaching of English mother-tongue, but not with EFL. EAL people do not feel part of the UK ELT industry. Neither does ELT particularly include them.

EAL has never interested ELT publishers, understandably, since there is no big market for materials. And it has been neglected by British universities. Three or four universities have begun to offer Master's degrees, which is a good thing; but these are not training courses and thus offer no remedy for the dearth of EAL training. This contrasts with the situation in the USA where English for minorities in schools has a high university profile and dominates the activity of the TESOL association.

English-medium education overseas

Let me now turn to the third of my categories of ESL: English-medium education overseas. By this I refer to those countries where education is provided through the medium of English as a second language either from the first day of primary school, or part-way through primary school, or at the beginning of secondary school. The main countries I am concerned with are those of post-colonial sub-Saharan Africa, but the category obviously includes other poor countries such as Bhutan and other rich countries such as Hong Kong or Brunei.

SCHOOL ROLE/SOCIETAL FUNCTION OF ENGLISH

These are contexts in which English serves a fairly wide range of societal functions and serves as a language of wider communication, but is not the language of the home or the street, or of other forms of local communication such as commerce.

EXPOSURE TO ENGLISH/ STATUS OF L1 OR COMMUNITY LANGUAGE

Exposure to English varies radically from fairly high in a place like Johannesburg to very low in, say, rural KwaZulu; low enough indeed for many to question whether English is viable as a MOI – a debate which is rife in Tanzania, for example. Home and community languages in these contexts are strong and will remain so. They usually play a role as MOI in the early years of schooling. Bilingualism is thus very much additive. However, education through the medium of English as a second language in African contexts is not working well and I have no doubt that one cause of economic under-development in English-medium sub-Saharan Africa is that education systems are not delivering the necessary levels of education, because these countries are having to face language barriers in education which the North would never dream of accepting.

The problem comes to a head in rural areas where children get little exposure to English. Here, literacy levels in the local MOI or English in the early years of primary school are often low. This is a fragile basis for educational success and it can then be perpetuated throughout a student's school career by low exposure to English, but also by insufficient levels of teacher education, poor resourcing, and above all the failure of the system to address head-on the problems inherent in trying to run an education service through the medium of what is really a second, third or fourth language for everyone in the classroom.

For many children, this means, for example, that children are inadequately prepared before a switch of MOI to use English for cognitive, literacy and curricular development. The switch hits them hard; dropout rates may be high at this point and while they are struggling to stand still in their English language development, the goal posts are moved and the curriculum begins to make huge and ever-increasing language demands on them. Teachers, as I have known them in South Africa for example, are impressive in what they achieve under the circumstances, but there is no hiding the fact that learning school subject-matter knowledge satisfactorily is often well-nigh impossible when neither teacher nor pupils can really speak English adequately to use it as a vehicle for giving or getting an education.

INTEGRATION WITH CURRICULUM

Under these circumstances, it is important for English teaching to be integrated as fully as possible into the teaching of the mainstream curriculum both in the early years and further up the school. What is needed in the early years is literacy. It should probably be L1 literacy, but it doesn't really matter in what language it is as long as children have a firm foundation of cognitive and literacy skills to enable them to handle the difficult business of using language for learning. So primary EFL will not do here: primary English should be strongly oriented to cognitive and literacy development across the curriculum in a multilingual setting (as it is, for example in the Molteno project in South Africa). Likewise, secondary EFL will also not do: it has to be teaching secondary subjects through the medium of English as a second language.

MODEL OF PEDAGOGY

One could say a lot about typical models of pedagogy in African English-medium classrooms, and this is indeed an important issue. But the more pressing question for ELT is whether those of its representatives who work in these education systems understand that it is the English-medium classroom, rather than the English language classroom which should chiefly concern us.

There has been a serious misunderstanding over many years both on the part of education authorities in English-medium countries and in external institutions involved in providing educational aid to them. It concerns the belief that what English-medium education systems need is an injection of expertise into the English language slot in the curriculum, that students will take their improved English skills into subject classrooms and that this will lift the efficiency of education across the curriculum. Now, everything we know about EAL in the UK and elsewhere – as well as our experience of education in English-medium systems in Africa – tells us that this will not work. The main thing we can do to improve the performance of the school system as a whole is to help mainstream teachers to teach their subject through English. Language teaching alone clearly has its uses; but improvements to the effectiveness of English teaching do not hit the spot: they catch on only in a patchy way; they do not easily cross subject boundaries; they do not often address cross-curricular issues; and crucially, they do not target the source of the problem, namely the failure of subject teachers to teach with the serious obstacles of L2-medium learning in mind.

Education authorities in the UK learned this long ago and 'mainstreamed' their EAL work; but many still expect separate-subject communicative language teaching to help African students to learn curricular subjects through English. In the past, we have poured good money after bad into the ELT slot in the curriculum, rather than funding the training of, say, science and maths teachers to negotiate the language barrier.

TRAINING OPPORTUNITIES

Training opportunities which address the need for English-medium subject teaching, rather than communicative EFL, are thin on the ground.

STATE OF HEALTH

English-medium education in Africa is in a poorer state of health than we would like to admit. Anyone who has been in Africa and looked at these issues – and many would rather not – has asked themselves whether it is possible to place on such under-resourced and overcrowded schools the huge extra burden of teaching through a language which most in the classroom, including the teacher, are struggling to use. I should make clear that I am certainly not saying that it can't be done. There is really no alternative in the short and medium term. What I am saying is that we have to realise that it is difficult. It requires teachers who are trained to integrate the acquisition of language and subject-matter knowledge and materials which do the same. That in turn requires expertise which training institutions and publishers can use.

ELT has not seriously addressed the question of generating such expertise.

ELT departments in the universities still believe that communicative EFL expertise is relevant and they have been active in providing it to aid-funded projects in Africa. Many in departments of overseas education, similarly, still think that you can do English-medium maths and science teaching in Africa without worrying too much about language. But I know of only very few departments who are developing expertise in teaching primary and secondary curricular contents through ESL.

Integrated maths, science and English projects have often come perforce to the conclusion that expertise in English-medium maths and science was necessary. Unfortunately, having established this rather late in the life of their project, they have found it difficult to find either consultancy expertise in this hybrid field or departments where they could send their local staff to learn about it. Lots of science and maths projects do, of course, do the right thing in the end and generate significant bodies of expertise in English-medium education, but they all end up reinventing their own wheels, in parallel, so to speak.

It is important that ELT learns to make common cause with primary and secondary curricular subject teaching and develop expertise which will be truly useful to hard-pressed English-medium teachers in Africa. The expertise exists, of course, in the British LEA language service teams, in one or two university departments, in the British Council in Hong Kong, for instance, and in German English-medium secondary schools. Europe and Africa are different contexts of course and one must be wary of the idea of transferring expertise. But the Hounslow Language Service in London, for example, has done excellent work in South Africa and Namibia.

Reasons for paying attention to ESL

Let me pull my argument together. I am saying that there are different strains of ESL which are important and I am proposing that they deserve more attention from ELT and from the institutions which constitute it. Why should they get more attention? There are two reasons. The first refers to our business to ensure that our field is academically coherent. The second refers to our duty as providers of educational services to ensure that we are informed.

The coherence of ELT theory and practice

The argument here goes like this: ESL exists; and is practised in many different contexts. ELT includes ESL and the academic study of ELT theory and practice must take account of it, if it is not to remain incomplete.

Assuming that research were to turn its attention solidly to primary and secondary curriculum-driven ESL as it is practised in any of my three contexts, to describe it, analyse it, evaluate, promote and improve it, what would it find that would be of interest? A hybrid practice, which ESL is, with one foot in ELT and the other in curriculum and cognition, throws up a multitude of interesting questions for research in ELT or language in education.

On language and cognition   What kinds of teacher-talk, or small-group talk help children learn school subjects? What are the key language and learning processes which constitute, for example, good science teaching or good geography teaching? And I should say in parenthesis here that ESL more than any other branch of teaching has developed the analysis of school language demands as a professional tool.

On task design   How do you design tasks for teaching subjects, which make high cognitive demands but low language demands? In other words, tasks which are both subject-learning and language-learning tasks? ESL teachers are extremely good at this kind of thing.

On second language acquisition   Isn't it interesting to find SLA which doesn't involve much controlled input and practice, selection and grading, presentation practice and production?

On the development of school language policy   What is the best way of getting a school collectively to undertake improvements in the way all teachers deal with language?

These are all key questions in language in education and language across the curriculum; questions at the heart of school learning. And I think ESL gets as close as any branch of teaching to providing answers.

The provision of ELT services

The second reason why ESL deserves more attention is because ELT provides services to clients: language teaching services, training services, research, advice and consultancy. Many of these services relate to the ESL contexts which I have been describing. We must be in a position to offer services which are appropriate to them.

   At present, I do not think that language schools, training institutions, universities, publishers, or information brokers would be able to provide adequate responses to many of the questions which clients in ESL contexts will bring them. For example:

- If I am from the Botswanan ministry of education I might ask (as I myself have been asked): what skills are needed by subject teachers in English-medium schools in Botswana, to ensure that education does not let down as many students as it might?

- If I am a field manager in a Namibian project providing aid to primary education there, where often in rural black schools, both teachers and children may struggle with English, I might ask: how can we ensure that in the early years of schooling children get a solid foundation of cognitive and literacy skills, because as it is, our rural schools are not functioning in English anything like well enough? What do you know about early literacy development in under-resourced multilingual settings which can help me?

- If I am a science or maths specialist going out to spend a lot of taxpayers' money on a maths and science aid project in English-medium Zambia, I might ask: what skills are needed by maths and science teachers so that they are effective in doing maths and science with students who have little English?

- If I am a Finnish ministerial official, receiving requests from schools wanting to teach through the medium of English, I might ask: where can I send groups of teachers who want to improve their ability to teach their subject through English?

- If I am an EU official from Brussels, concerned that 'plurilingual education' in European schools fulfils the promise that is claimed for it, I might ask: which universities are engaged in research and training in English-medium education in secondary schools, because we want to approach them for advice?

- If I am from DFID, thinking about education in sub-Saharan Africa and pursuing my most recently established policy of 'encouraging a cross-curricular approach to the teaching of core subjects such as mathematics, science and language; and training teachers of other subjects in the effective use of language for learning' (DFID 1998), I am likely to ask: where can I find expertise in doing just this?

Responding to the issue

How could ELT respond most usefully to ESL in its various guises? I will suggest a few ideas very briefly.

Awareness

Firstly various sectors of ELT need to recognise that ESL is significant and becoming more so. Higher education and cultural agencies should acknowledge that there is an information gap here; they should get informed about ESL, ask questions about it, establish the demand for it and begin to shape its development. Above all, they need to find out where the expertise is currently located.

Matching need with expertise

Secondly, it is important to recognise and categorise types of educational need accurately and to match them with appropriate expertise. In Africa, for instance, it is certainly important for agencies and universities to stop misdiagnosing needs as communicative language teaching problems and recognise the need for early literacy and English-medium science and maths skills. And then they need to match these needs with the expertise in these fields which we have in ESL.

Links to other subjects

Thirdly, it is important to recognise that ESL is a hybrid form of ELT. You can't do it unless you connect with expertise in the teaching of the primary and secondary curriculum. EAP has a similar connection to tertiary subject contents. There are new things which ELT has to learn here and it isn't difficult to make the leap. University ELT and education departments, for instance, are often just next door to each other.

Links between ESL and EFL

Fourthly, there are obviously links to be made between ESL and EFL institutions, between associations, conferences and journals.

Developing expertise

Finally, ESL expertise needs developing. Universities have recently begun researching EAL. They should also be developing expertise in, say, bilingual education or early literacy development for English-medium Africa, or English-medium science teaching in Africa; there are lots of fields crying out for research.

And lastly, in case you still don't believe me, let me quote David Graddol (1997:14):

> An important community for the future development of English in the world is …
> those who speak it as a second language. English often plays a special role in their
> lives and the fate of English in the world is likely to be closely connected to how
> this role develops in future.

7 Teaching English through Content: Supporting Good Practice

Jean Brewster
Thames Valley University, London

In the UK, attempts to implement language development alongside subject learning led to a wide range of classroom materials, publications and teachers' courses under the banner of 'language across the curriculum' (see DES Bullock Report, 1975). Most of these tried to incorporate a particular view of language and learning processes, transferable across subjects, which subsequently underpinned the teaching of students for whom English is an additional language (EAL). More recently, secondary schools throughout Europe have also encouraged the integration of language and content learning. This has provided a springboard for innovative pedagogy, leading to a growing number of publications and networks between teachers in their attempt to understand and develop the principles and practice for effective teaching of English across the curriculum (EAC). (See Clegg, this volume.) Based on extensive experience with UK teachers teaching English as an additional language and EAC teachers from Austria and France, this paper will consider three key questions:

- What is the rationale for EAC in Europe?
- What models can EAC teacher education provide to promote good practice?
- How can we work with European partners to disseminate good practice?

The rationale for EAC

Some years ago Widdowson wrote that:

> a foreign language can be associated with those areas of use which are represented by the other subjects on the school curriculum... this not only helps to ensure the link with reality and the pupil's own experience but also provides us with the most certain means we have of teaching the language as communication, as use, rather than simply as usage (Widdowson, 1978:16).

Additionally, integrating language with content is commonly justified by reference to arguments such as those proposed by Snow, Met and Genesee (1992).

- Traditional methods for teaching second languages often disassociate learning from cognitive or academic development.

- Language is learned most effectively for communication in meaningful, purposeful, social and academic contexts.
- Integration of language and content provides a substantive basis for language teaching and learning; content can provide a motivational and cognitive basis for language learning since it is interesting and of some value to the learner.
- The language of different subject areas is characterised by specific genres or registers which may be a prerequisite of specific content or to academic development in general.

The Austrian Education Act of 1986 encouraged an increasing number of 'bilingual' schools to teach foreign languages across the curriculum, especially where it 'seems to serve the purpose of improving education in a foreign language and does not prejudice the general accessibility of the individual formats and subject directions of different types of school.' The wish of bilingual schools to develop individual profiles for 'Englisch als Arbeitssprache' is seen as a means of intensifying foreign language teaching, achieving substantial improvement in linguistic competence and even creating 'additive' bilingualism depending on the intensity of teaching. Subjects where English is used include history, geography and biology.

In France some bilingual classes were first set up in secondary schools in the 1970s where PE or Art was taught in the L2. For the academic year 1992, under the auspices of the 'European Sections', a larger number of schools began teaching subjects (similar to those in Austria) in a variety of foreign languages such as English, German, Spanish and Italian. In 1996 there were 152 European Sections in French lycées, 68 of which use English as the target language. According to Pernet (1996) the objectives of this programme are twofold: firstly, to develop the linguistic competence of pupils by providing a longer period of exposure to the target language and secondly to give students an in-depth knowledge of the country or countries where the language is spoken as the mother tongue. Pernet writes that the European Sections in France have had a highly beneficial effect on language learning in secondary schools on several counts: teachers have better relations with their pupils, barriers between subjects have been removed, teachers are increasingly reassessing their teaching methods, pupil-centred learning is on the increase.

There are at least two major European centres for promoting EAC: the first, the *European Centre for Modern Languages*, established with European Union funding in Graz, Austria, has a flourishing LAC network, linking teachers from Austria, Latvia, the Netherlands, Poland, Romania and the Ukraine. Activities include conferences, newsletter and materials production (see e.g. Kolodziejska *et al.*, 1997). The second, the *European Network for Plurilingual Education*, based in the Netherlands, links teachers from thirteen countries with a newsletter, conferences and a web site. Interesting developments in EAC have also sprung up in several other countries such as Hong Kong and South Africa. However, as yet there is a scarcity of research on the impact of EAC on both teachers and students in all of these countries.

Promoting 'good practice' in teacher education

The views of UK trainers who work with EAC teachers in Europe are usually based on practice and research drawn from a wide range of sources, chiefly within the UK, USA, Canada and Australia. In this paper I shall refer to four main areas which inform teacher education practice for EAC contexts.

- Cross-curricular methods: how to plan for language and content integration;
- Task-based, collaborative learning: how students use language to learn;
- Support techniques: how teachers use talk and other means to teach;
- Principles and practice for EAC materials design.

Language and content integration

In EAC approaches the teacher's task is to resolve some of the tensions between gaining access to the curriculum and language acquisition. Cross-curricular methods recognise the interdependence of language and learning (see e.g. Clegg, 1996 and this volume; Corson, 1990; Cummins, 1984; Gibbons, 1991; Marland, 1977; Wells and Chang-Wells, 1992). Additionally, cross-curricular approaches aim to provide:

- integrated planning for both language inputs and outputs with explicit language and curriculum outcomes;
- opportunities for interaction using all four skills;
- exposure to appropriate models;
- contextualised access to the curriculum content without automatic simplification of the concepts.

An important stage in EAC planning is the need to analyse pupils' linguistic and educational needs and match these to subject-specific content demands; areas in which students require support can then be ascertained. Where language and learning demands are analysed side by side there are greater opportunities to plan for the transfer of skills and for operating at the level of discourse, not simply sentence or word level (see Cameron *et al.*, 1996 for more on how EAL pupils respond to classroom learning demands). The output required, the kinds of tasks used and their concomitant demands are analysed in order that a framework of appropriate support and intervention can be provided where necessary. Teachers are then able to establish both language and learning objectives (for examples of how planning and materials design was achieved in a national scheme for EAL teacher education in the UK see Brewster, 1992).

Snow, Met and Genesee (1992) propose a framework where teachers determine teaching objectives which derive from two considerations: 'content-obligatory' and 'content-compatible' language. The former is closely associated with specific content objectives and is almost impossible not to use. It tends to consist of both structural items such as verbs, nouns, tenses and functional items or skills, for instance hypothesising or note-taking. When studying the topic of volcanoes in geography, for example, content obligatory language might include verbs such as 'erupt, force, melt', nouns such as 'magma, core, lava' and functions such as the language for expressing cause and effect using verbs such as 'causes', 'leads to', 'results in', and cohesive devices such as 'consequently', 'therefore', 'as a result'. Content compatible functions might include recycling language learned previously, for example, describing a process using 'first, then, next, finally, the first stage' and so on. These language objectives may be drawn from three sources: the general language syllabus which takes account of pupils' continuing growth and development; the teacher's observation of student language skills and analysis of needs; and the anticipated or long range linguistic demands of content curriculum to be taught in future lessons. During INSET teachers can be encouraged to analyse the linguistic demands of an activity by completing charts with headings such as concepts to be learned, key language skills, functions, vocabulary and sentence patterns (see e.g. Gibbons, 1991:ch. 2). Having analysed the demands of a topic, the teacher is encouraged to provide 'scaffolding' for each stage by means of structured activities, the use of visual aids or hands on experience. One aim of training is to widen the repertoire of activities teachers call upon, so that, for example, they focus on discourse structure as well as specialised vocabulary.

So far we have seen how EAC teachers need to develop an ability to examine potential subject content in order to pinpoint and highlight the underlying conceptual frameworks and discourse types used and the content compatible or content obligatory language required. Additionally, teachers need to understand how language inputs can be planned together with language outcomes in order to realise the curriculum learning aims of the content areas.

How students use language to learn

The importance of learning through interaction using group work and pair work has been advocated in mainstream education (see e.g. Barnes and Todd, 1977; Mercer, 1995) while in English language learning contexts studies such as Long and Porter (1985) or Swain (1995) demonstrate the need for collaborative learning in order to support students' ability to verbalise content knowledge. Research shows that collaborative learning methods can improve the effectiveness of student learning in content-integrated classrooms (see e.g. McGroarty, 1992), while in second-language classes the quantity and quality of student talk can be increased (Long and Porter, 1985).

EAC approaches require teachers to select content from the school's curriculum that is compatible with the school's language objectives so that the content becomes cognitively engaging. A focus on the pupils' linguistic outputs i.e. those expected as a result of the learning aims and those expected by planned classroom activities, is an increasingly well recognised stage of language learning (Swain, 1995). Using these approaches, students are encouraged to make active use of language for genuine communicative purposes involving a variety of discourse types. Thus teacher talk, listening and reading tasks and a variety of pupil outputs in spoken or written form build up content knowledge which simultaneously draw on appropriate language, ascertained by the pupils' needs and the curriculum content demands (see Clegg 1996 for examples of the application of these kinds of framework in lesson plans at both secondary and primary levels).

Context-sensitive teacher talk and other support

The ways in which teachers use talk and support materials in language and content teaching is of crucial significance. Cummins stresses the importance of taking account of the function and content of teacher talk (TT) to ascertain what is appropriate and useful. For example, with regard to questioning and typical classroom exchanges (initiation, response, feedback/IRF) he writes, 'There are ways of using questions and IRF exchanges which are more appropriate and useful than others' (1981:33). Both Cummins (1981) and Met (1994) refer to the importance of 'context-embedded' teacher talk as a means of making sense of and creating continuity in the students' learning experiences.

This can be achieved in the first instance by linking new learning to background knowledge, secondly by means of 'scaffolding' to make language inputs comprehensible, for example, using contextual clues such as realia, demonstrations, 'knowledge frameworks' and 'key visuals', such as flowcharts and diagrams (see Hooper, 1996; Mohan, 1986; Tang, 1992). Finally, teachers make their language more comprehensible by modifying their speech e.g. speaking more slowly, emphasising key words and phrases, using simpler vocabulary or grammar, building in redundancy through repeating, restating, paraphrasing, the use of synonyms, antonyms, defining through exemplification, body language and so on. Wong-Fillmore (1985, 1989) highlights the need for clear teacher roles and teacher language, while Clegg (1994) refers to ten dimensions for measuring a 'facilitative teaching style' in EAL contexts. These include comprehensible teacher talk, the promotion of interaction through task-focused small group work, clear task purpose and orderly task sequences. EAC teachers must decide how far these characteristics are suitable for their lessons.

Context-embedded support

In EAC contexts pupils need to develop the English required for higher order cognitive skills since they are likely to deploy more complex or elaborate language skills and more challenging tasks than in traditional EFL classrooms. The work of Mohan and colleagues in Vancouver (e.g. Hooper, 1996; Tang, 1992) argues that the use of a 'knowledge framework' and concomitant 'key visuals' leads to effective, context-embedded support. Knowledge frameworks outline six categories of activity within educational settings which reflect the range of background knowledge (classification, principles and evaluation) and practical knowledge (description, sequence and choice) that learners encounter when they are exposed to content knowledge. The tables in the appendix (page 93ff) illustrate the use of the knowledge framework and key visuals in the topic *Local Industry in Hounslow* (Thorley, 1994) as used with EAL students in the UK.

Stretching, expanding and refining students' language

In integrated language and content classes students need to check their growing linguistic repertoire, fluency and confidence. Teachers may do this in several ways, firstly by encouraging students to draw upon context-embedded techniques similar to those they have modelled in the input stages. For example, students can make use of key visuals or writing frames in the planning and production stages of written or spoken outputs. Secondly teachers can make 'rich interpretations' of students' attempts to communicate by expanding students' responses (see Wells, 1986), using comprehension checks, or by teaching 'achievement strategies' for conversational management (Faerch and Kasper, 1983). Where students are given opportunities to become active users of educated forms of discourse, they require training in the collaborative skills required to work on tasks without the teacher's constant intervention and control.

Implications for good practice in teacher education

As we have seen, teachers must attend to their effectiveness in creating continuity and coherence in their students' educational experience. They also need to give careful consideration to how they 'scaffold' their students' active participation in academic discourse. Thus, the goal of INSET should be not only to provide teachers with an increased awareness of the principles outlined above but also to provide them with opportunities to extend their repertoire of teaching styles, modes and activities and how to make informed choices about the selection of these options.

We can now summarise the skills a training course for EAC teachers needs to develop:

- the ability to analyse the linguistic and cognitive demands of lessons, to plan language and learning objectives and match these to pupils' needs;
- the capacity to analyse the language use required for tasks in terms of skills or strategies which need to be modelled by the teacher or peers; to provide practice for this language in purposeful contexts which arise naturally out of the general learning activities;
- the ability to draw upon their knowledge about language or language processes (e.g. cohesion in texts or the importance of prediction in listening) and to use this knowledge when designing activities;
- an understanding of the principles and practice of using a wide variety of activities which offer support for learning at appropriate levels;
- the capacity to stage activities so that each one draws upon skills and language developed in previous activities so as to provide task continuity;
- an understanding of the management of learning with regard to due factors such as organising and monitoring groups, thus facilitating independent learning.

Although courses exist in various countries which aim to cover some of the above, there is, as yet, little systematic in-depth teacher education for EAC teachers.

Materials design

Many EAC teachers with whom I have worked refer to the dearth of motivating subject-specific materials which systematically integrate language and content at a range of levels. Until such materials are widely available teachers also need to develop an understanding of the principles and practice of materials design. In participating countries some EAC materials have recently been developed by teachers under the auspices of the Language Across the Curriculum Network. In Austria and Germany, to cite two examples, there are published content-specific materials (see the *English Across the Curriculum* series: Kuchl and

Simpson, 1995 and also Biederstädt, 1993). A key issue in published materials design is the use of local or international textbooks. Newby (1997) writes of the need 'to strengthen the confidence that (local) authors and publishers should rightly feel in their own ability and materials' .

Many teachers of EAC make use of resources and materials for English native speakers in secondary schools. In this case, teachers must decide how far to simplify the language without oversimplifying the concepts or content (decisions regarding the appropriacy of the content is another factor). The required language may be pre-taught, elicited from more linguistically competent students, or provided as the need arises. Visual support, such as realia, videos, CD-ROMs along with key visuals or knowledge frameworks help to make the discourse structure explicit. Tasks must then be designed which encourage students to become active learners and producers of the language; this helps to counteract a tendency for some teachers to place students in a more passive role. An example of a language framework which provides content-obligatory lexis is shown below.

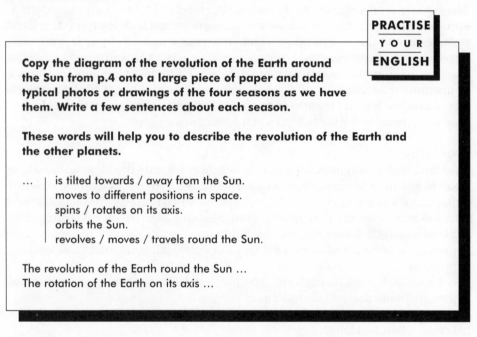

PRACTISE
Y O U R
ENGLISH

Copy the diagram of the revolution of the Earth around the Sun from p.4 onto a large piece of paper and add typical photos or drawings of the four seasons as we have them. Write a few sentences about each season.

These words will help you to describe the revolution of the Earth and the other planets.

...	is tilted towards / away from the Sun.
	moves to different positions in space.
	spins / rotates on its axis.
	orbits the Sun.
	revolves / moves / travels round the Sun.

The revolution of the Earth round the Sun ...
The rotation of the Earth on its axis ...

from *Around the World: The Earth in Space* (Biederstädt, 1993) 5

This language illustrates Mohan's categories of description and sequence (practical knowledge) and principles (background knowledge). These patterns contain the language functions of describing position and explaining a process with use of the present tense and the passive; if the latter were learned previously these functions may be regarded as exponents of content-compatible language, while specialised lexis such as 'axis, tilts, rotates, orbits' are exponents of content-obligatory language. Tasks such as these must be ordered and graded in such a way as to provide continuity and coherence. In developing reading and speaking skills tasks might include DARTS (directed activities related towards texts) such as sequencing, predicting, information transfer and various types of information gap (see Lunzer and Gardner, 1984); written outputs might be supported by a speaking and reading activity and the provision of a writing frame (see Wray and Lewis, 1997). Thus an important part of the materials design process in teacher education is the widening of teachers' repertoire of task types which develop all four skills. Let us examine this more closely.

Materials design components on teacher education courses

Teacher education courses or workshops for EAC frequently have a materials design component which encapsulates both process and product dimensions. As Kiely writes, 'The process dimension develops and extends teachers' competence by requiring them to consider a complex array of linguistic and curricular needs and demands in relation to a variety of contextual factors' (1996:60). These factors, he suggests, might include the needs of school curricula, current approaches to language teaching and classroom methodology, the teachers' own needs and the contribution which materials can make to their work. The development of teacher-made materials packs acts as a catalyst, encouraging teachers to combine theory with practice while providing a highly motivating course outcome. Additionally, many teachers report a boost to their professional confidence and competence since they have acquired useful, transferable skills suitable for other topics and colleagues.

Implications

Materials design components can help teachers identify the language learning potential of the core activity of a classroom task, construct clear goals, select suitable task sequences from a (perhaps widened) repertoire of tasks, and develop strategies for maximising students' language use and learning. Key skills in materials design include the ability to:
- identify important tasks and task types in curriculum, materials and learning processes;
- enhance task work by exploring co-operative learning, strategic learning and the functional analysis of discourse;
- explore the relationships between tasks and their relationship to learning of both content and language;
- evaluate language and learning processes, firstly by reference to the materials' effectiveness in meeting the stated objectives and secondly by reference to the pupils' actual language performance which reveals the extent to which their language and learning needs were met.

This last point refers to evaluation of the product dimension of the component – the materials. However, Kiely (1996) also stresses the need for 'developmental evaluation' of the materials writing process after the materials have been made or even trialled. Such evaluation might include the following set of questions, useful for both teachers and teacher educators to reflect upon:

- How useful was the materials writing process?
- What were the most important insights you gained?
- How were the materials used?
- Should the materials have specified timing or not?
- Should they have a specified sequence of tasks or built-in flexibility?
- What aspects worked particularly well/badly?
- How much were they modified and why?
- Have other colleagues tried them?
- What was the impact of the materials on the pupils and other teachers?

The extent of this type of action research is limited at the moment but would provide a fruitful avenue of inquiry.

How can we work with European partners to disseminate good practice?

An important consideration in the conceptualisation of good practice is the tension created between generalisability and context-specificity; that is, to what extent can aspects of good practice carry across a variety of contexts and how far is good practice context-specific? The model discussed in this paper is process rather than product-oriented; its appropriacy will vary from context to context. Nevertheless, contacts between EAC and EAL teachers or modern language teachers, across a wide range of contexts and with differing commitments to process and product-oriented views of teaching, may be fruitful.

Obstacles EAC teachers need to overcome

So far we have highlighted the scarcity of good materials and resources and rather limited provision of specialised EAC training. Teachers' language proficiency may also be a factor where they are subject specialists rather than language specialists. An additional problem concerns working practices and the role of the teacher. In immersion teaching in majority English-language speaking countries there is often collaboration or 'partnership' teaching between language specialists and content teachers. In European contexts these roles are fused, although there is often some form of collaboration with native-speakers who may plan lessons jointly, or provide help with English language or materials design. However, in many contexts teachers tend to work in isolation from their fellow colleagues rather than in teams; teachers in an EAC workshop in Austria reported this tradition. This can make networking with colleagues within and across schools difficult or even unwelcome since it is perceived (rightly) as time-consuming. The materials design process may become onerous since it is carried out in professional isolation. Recently local INSET courses in Austria have established regional networks in order that members can develop a sense of collegiality with all the benefits this can provide.

Researching good practice

Another promising avenue may be to adapt research questions concerning good practice in EAL (Cameron and Leung, 1998) which raise the kinds of issue which are relevant to EAC contexts. Here are ten areas which may be a useful starting point.

What is good practice?
- What does it look like in different contexts?
- Who decides what is good practice? How much teacher autonomy is there in deciding this?
- What kinds of principle underpin successful approaches to integrated language and content teaching and learning? Are they universal?
- How do we know classroom practice is 'good': from teachers; from pupils; from examination results? What might be better that is not current practice?
- How do English language tasks relate to the rest of the curriculum?
- How can English language tasks with a curricular focus be graded?
- How far should new concepts and content at secondary level be taught in the mother tongue?
- To what extent should English act as a vehicle to teach content or be the focus of an activity where content is a secondary aim?
- To what extent is curriculum content watered down to match the linguistic level of the students and/or the teachers? Is this a problem?

Such research, drawing on a variety of techniques, such as journals, interviews, video-based data or stimulated recall, has the potential to inform practice and influence or even challenge EAC policies. Ideally it should be responsive to such policies, foster research as a way of thinking amongst practitioners and be responsive to questions from practitioners.

Conclusions

Teachers and teacher educators in Europe are learning to overcome the problems of developing and disseminating good practice in EAC which, this paper has argued, can learn much from insights gained in the last two decades from contexts where English is the medium of instruction. Since an increasing number of pupils in Europe are now learning English in primary schools there may be a problem with providing sufficient challenge and interest for pupils when they move to secondary school. 'More of the same' is unlikely to retain sustained interest for all students. An integrated, process-oriented approach to content and language teaching, as described in this paper, aims to engage students fully with interesting and cognitively challenging activities. Thus a systematic approach to EAC teaching may provide interesting opportunities for students to engage in purposeful and motivating language learning.

Acknowledgements
I am indebted to Paul Thorley and Manny Vasquez for allowing me to reproduce part of their material.

Appendix: Local Industry in Hounslow (Thorley, 1994)

The Knowledge Framework 1: Thinking Skills

CLASSIFICATION/CONCEPTS	PRINCIPLES	EVALUATION
Types of Industry	**The distribution of employment**	**The impact of re-development**
Classification Industry is divided into primary, secondary and tertiary. *Definition* e.g. primary industry – uses things from the earth. *Exemplification* e.g. primary industry – farming, fishing, mining, forestry.	*Interpreting data and drawing conclusions* e.g. a high proportion of people in Hounslow work in transport due to the proximity of Heathrow airport.	*Judging and ranking* Examining the positive and negative effects of re-development and deciding on their relative importance.
The location of industry in Hounslow	**The growth of industrial activity**	**Choosing the location of an economic activity**
Describing location	*Time relations between events and their causes* e.g. The Great West Road was built in the 1920's due to traffic congestion in Brentford.	*Making decisions* Choosing the most suitable location for an industry.
DESCRIPTION	SEQUENCE	CHOICE

The Knowledge Framework 2: Key Visuals

CLASSIFICATION/CONCEPTS	PRINCIPLES	EVALUATION

Key Visuals

Classification tree

Key Visuals

Divided Bar Graph showing the distribution of employment

Key Visuals

Evaluation Grid

	Impact	+ or –	Rank
office block, etc.	3000 jobs	+	

Key Visuals

Map of Hounslow showing the location of industry

Key Visuals

Date, Event and Cause Table

Date	Event	Cause
1920's	Gt West Road was built	Traffic congestion in Brentford

Key Visuals

Advantages Table

Advantages of Hounslow	Advantages of South Wales

DESCRIPTION	SEQUENCE	CHOICE

The Knowledge Framework 3: Language

CLASSIFICATION/CONCEPTS	PRINCIPLES	EVALUATION
Vocabulary Primary, secondary, tertiary, manufacturing, distribution, public service, transport, office work, mining, fishing, farming, forestry. **Grammar** Present simple e.g. Transport includes working on railways or at an airport	**Vocabulary** Primary, secondary, tertiary, transport, manufacturing, distribution, public service, office work. **Grammar** Present simple/passive e.g. The graph shows .... people .... are employed .... **Cause:** This is because	**Expressing Opinion** I think that .... should/not have been demolished because .... **Evaluating** The most/least important effect is .... The good/bad effects are ....
Vocabulary East, west, central, along, close to, just to, on. **Grammar** Present passive e.g. Heathrow Airport is located just to the west of Hounslow.	**Grammar** Past passive e.g. Firestone tyre factory was built .... **Cause:** As a result of because as	**Expressing Opinion** I think/believe that .... should be located .... because ....
DESCRIPTION	SEQUENCE	CHOICE

8 More than an Act of Faith? Evaluating Learner Autonomy

Barbara Sinclair
University of Nottingham

The language teaching profession has made great progress in the exploration and implementation of the promotion of learner autonomy. This has led to a focus on what some have called 'learner training' in language courses, published materials, teacher training programmes and conference themes in much of the world. The establishment of self-access and learner resource centres, the increase in distance learning programmes and a growing involvement of information technology in language teaching all bear witness to this professional concern with empowering learners to be more effective and more independent in their learning.

Although a large number of language teaching professionals agree that developing these abilities is important and are enthusiastic about promoting learner autonomy, there remains one important question which has yet to be answered: does it really work? In other words, what evidence is there that programmes of learner training really do help learners to become more proficient and independent in their learning? Is the promotion of learner autonomy more than simply an act of faith?

Seeking evidence

There are four principal ways in which evidence to support the promotion of autonomy in language learning has been sought: by monitoring learners' proficiency gains in the target language, by collecting feedback from teachers and learners, by logging learner behaviour, and through research studies into the effects of strategy training.

Proficiency gains

The measurement of language learning success, i.e. gains in language proficiency, has been carried out by more 'traditional' means of assessment by teachers, as well as by encouraging learners to evaluate their own performances. Seeking this type of proof seems a sensible path to take since developing greater independence in learning is of little benefit unless it culminates in successful language learning; learner training aims to increase not only learners' independence, but also their effectiveness in learning (Ellis and Sinclair, 1989:2).

Generally, there seems to have been little research into the effects of promoting autonomy (through 'learner training' or 'strategy training') on learners' proficiency gains. However, one interesting example is the work of Green and Oxford, who report that strategies involving the active use of the target language, along with practice in naturalistic situations, were the most significant factors in the development of proficiency in a foreign language (Green and Oxford, 1995).

Results emerging from comparative studies in Denmark and Germany into vocabulary gains in beginning learners of English (Dam and Legenhausen, 1996) indicate the possible superiority of programmes promoting learner autonomy. In their article, Dam and Legenhausen describe an attempt to compare the vocabulary acquisition of twenty-one twelve-year-old, mixed ability, Danish beginning learners of English, who learnt in what they call 'the autonomous way', with two groups of similar students in Denmark and Germany, who learnt in a more 'traditional way' with textbooks. The vocabulary selected and publicly shared by the Danish autonomous group of learners was systematically recorded and its retention tested after seven and a half and fifteen weeks. The range, number and class of words retained was compared with those retained by the other two groups. The Danish autonomous learners retained a greater number of words, though were less orthographically correct than the Germans. Dam and Legenhausen do not, however, claim that their research is really able to make valid comparisons, since there were a number of important differences between the Danish and German groups, such as the coursebooks used and the different vocabulary presented in them, the proficiency levels of the students and the number of lessons per week. Nevertheless, they do suggest that their research demonstrates convincingly that 'vocabulary acquisition in the autonomous approach is very successful and compares favourably with results from more traditional textbook-based approaches' (Dam and Legenhausen, 1996:280).

Apart from these examples, however, there has been little evidence to suggest that learners who have followed a programme which promotes greater learner responsibility develop greater language proficiency than those who do not. It should be noted, though, that the length of time spent on the training may be important. To expect gains in proficiency in the short term may be unrealistic. Nevertheless, if the evaluation of the promotion of autonomy were based solely on reported proficiency gains of the learners involved, it would have to be concluded that teaching in this way is largely a waste of time. So why is it that many teachers and learners feel so strongly that students benefit from learner training?

Feedback from teachers and learners

Other sources of evidence of success in the promotion of learner autonomy come from feedback from the teacher and the learners; reports from teachers typically cite their students' increased levels of motivation, enthusiasm and active involvement in learning. For example, a Turkish primary school teacher using learner training techniques for the first time, reports that:

> They participate more, they ask more questions ... They feel confident and happy (Ellis, this volume).

There is a growing body of such subjective data which cannot be ignored. The collection of learner feedback in particular can provide useful, primary data on student attitudes and motivation. For example, Nunan (1997) reports on a study to investigate the effects of strategy training on sixty first-year undergraduates at the University of Hong Kong, who were randomly assigned to control and experimental groups. The experimental groups were systematically trained in fifteen learning strategies. Effects of this strategy training on four 'key aspects of the learning process' were assessed, including student motivation. He found a significant difference in student motivation for learning English between the experimental and the control groups, with the experimental group reporting a greater increase in motivation. (Other areas investigated were students' knowledge of strategies, the perceived utility of the strategies and actual deployment of the strategies by the students. The experimental groups significantly outperformed the control groups in all aspects listed above, except for deployment, for which there was no significant difference between the groups.)

However, there are two problems with feedback from learners and teachers. Firstly, researchers are still debating the relative status and acceptability of learner self-report data and evidence which might be considered valuable by some researchers may be disregarded by others. Secondly, notwithstanding debates on research methodology, there appears to be no proof so far, from empirical or qualitative research, that levels of motivation and learner involvement are caused *exclusively* by the promotion of autonomy in the course. This is hardly surprising given the number of variables that would be involved in such research; recent studies of motivation, for example, provide evidence of a highly complex, multi-faceted construct (Dörnyei, 1994; Gardner and MacIntyre, 1991; and Gardner and Tremblay, 1994). However, what teachers report from their classrooms seems to be the increased satisfaction of their students – a highly welcome development which should not be disregarded, but not one which necessarily demonstrates that they have become more effective and independent learners as a result.

Logging student activity

A common way of 'evaluating' autonomy, particularly in self-access learning contexts, is to log and monitor student behaviours. Students are typically required to keep logs or records of what learning tasks they have done, when they did them and how long they spent doing them. They may also be required to comment on the activity or assess their performance and identify problems. What evidence do such records, however, really provide about the development of autonomy? Often students record their written comments in as economical a manner as possible. It is not at all uncommon to see student logs with nothing but 'okay' written into the comments or assessment columns. Occasionally, students do write more, but even then, the comments tend to be minimal and, if written in the target language, constrained additionally by a lack of linguistic proficiency. Great care needs to be exercised in the interpretation of the evidence provided by student logs.

Experiments in strategy training

Further evidence of success in the promotion of learner autonomy has been sought by research studies of language learner strategies, for example, (Cohen, Weaver *et al.* 1995; and Oxford, 1990). Empirical evidence has been sought as to the trainability of language learning strategies and their effect on learning success and autonomy. For example, O'Malley *et al.* (1985b) investigated the effects of different kinds of strategy training, i.e., metacognitive, cognitive and socioaffective strategies, on different language skills. They found that training had a significant effect on speaking, but, interestingly, not on listening. Later, O'Malley and Chamot (1990) report that students identified by their teachers as more effective used strategies more and used a greater variety of strategies than less effective learners.

Often, such experimental findings may be counter-intuitive to many practitioners; for example, what is meant by using strategies 'more'? Do not all students use strategies all the time, whether consciously or subconsciously? Perhaps effective learners are more *aware* of the strategies they use. Similarly, might it not be the case that effective learners are likely to have discovered the strategies that work best for them and use them appropriately? For some this might mean a fairly small repertoire of nevertheless highly efficient strategies, rather than a broad variety of strategies. As Nunan (1997) has said, investigations of the effects of strategy training are still relatively rare and the results are somewhat inconclusive.

Some studies may be criticised both for their underlying assumptions about the nature of learner strategies and for the research methodology they employ: firstly, such studies may assume that it is possible to identify strategies which are useful for *everyone* to acquire. This concept of universally 'good' strategies may be true where receptive language skills are concerned; for example, it is generally agreed that learners of English benefit from being able to read in 'chunks' when reading for gist, and that they should learn to recognise stressed words when listening to spoken English for gist. However, the choice of strategies for other key areas of language learning, such as speaking, vocabulary learning and dealing with grammar, appear to be far more personal and affected by a greater variety of variables. Is it, therefore, valid to make assumptions about what strategies will work for individual students? Secondly, is it realistic to seek empirical evidence for such personal constructs? When students in research experiments demonstrate the use of the specific strategies chosen for training, are they really providing data that is meaningful in terms of the development of learner autonomy? A student may demonstrate that he/she can perform a certain strategy, but how does the researcher really know that he/she did not know this strategy before training and, perhaps, discounted it for valid personal reasons? How does the researcher know that the student is not trying to give the result the researcher is looking for? To summarise, training a student in a particular strategy cannot, in itself, guarantee that the student will add it to his or her repertoire of regularly used strategies, nor that it will be a personally suitable strategy for that particular student and enhance his/her learning success or ability to learn independently.

Notwithstanding these problems of underlying assumptions and research methodology, training learners in strategies does, however, have an important part to play in developing autonomy. Strategy training (or more broadly targeted 'learner training') provides opportunities for learners to increase their awareness of the learning processes available to them (Nunan, 1997). The development of such awareness is crucial to the development of learner autonomy and, as this paper will argue, is the basis for its evaluation.

Conclusion

It is possible to find limited evidence that learners who are able to learn independently may also gain greater proficiency. There are reports which describe the outcomes of learner training programmes in terms of learner satisfaction, increased motivation, more positive attitudes towards language learning, and greater enthusiasm. Some learner strategies have been identified which may increase learning effectiveness in most learners, and there is some evidence to suggest that strategies can be taught to students. However, none of this evidence, in itself, is a strongly compelling argument for promoting autonomy in language learning.

Although none of the previously discussed sources of evidence alone can provide the proof we seek, it would be a mistake, nevertheless, to discount them wholly. Rather, they may be regarded as an important part of the background to a differently targeted framework for evaluation. At present, though, there is no such framework for the evaluation of learner autonomy. Teachers, course planners and materials writers are left to do what they think is best, to rely on their own beliefs about learning, their values, experience and intuition. None of these things should be derided. However, those who believe that they have found a way to empower their learners are left open to criticism by researchers and teachers seeking evidence. In addition, there are real problems in selecting appropriate research methodologies to investigate links between the promotion of autonomy and gains in levels of independence in the learners. Perhaps the time has come when a different view of the evaluation of learner autonomy should be taken. In order to do so, it is necessary to look again at what is meant by 'learner autonomy'.

Defining autonomy in language learning

There have been many useful definitions of autonomy, Holec (1981:5), the Bergen definition (Dam, 1995) and Little (1991), amongst others. For example, Holec defines autonomy as 'the ability to take charge of one's own learning', and explains as follows: 'To take charge of one's own learning is to have, and to hold, the responsibility for all the decisions concerning all aspects of this learning.' He elucidates further with a crucial point: 'Autonomy is thus a term describing a potential capacity to act in a given situation – in our case – learning, and not the actual behaviour of an individual in that situation' (Holec, 1981:5).

It is interesting to note that, with respect to autonomy in language learning, current understandings of the concept refer to a capacity or ability to make informed decisions about one's learning, rather than actual behaviour or freedom from constraint. This has important implications for the evaluation of autonomy. Is it possible to rely on observable phenomena in order to judge whether a learner is developing greater autonomy? Consider this scenario:

> Mario, a student of business and Management English, is working in the self-access centre. He is attempting a reading comprehension activity based on a journal article about the effects of cultural values on the workplace which he has selected from a bank of available materials. So far, he is getting on quite well. He notices, however, a term which appears regularly, seems important, but which baffles him, i.e. 'power distance'. He knows the two constituent words, but cannot work out what the collocation means in this context. He gets up from his chair and approaches the tutor on duty in the self-access centre and asks her what it means.

Is Mario demonstrating autonomy or not? The casual observer, or the tutor, might feel that Mario is taking the easy, teacher-dependent way out. How does the tutor know, however, that Mario did not spend a considerable amount of time trying to figure out the meaning of the term from the context on his own first? How does the tutor know that he did not consider using the dictionaries in the self-access centre to help him unravel the problem, but dismissed that as a possible solution because a) it could mean looking at several dictionaries to arrive at an understanding b) there is no specific Management English dictionary available in the self-access centre c) it would all take too long and he is keen to continue with his activity. He may know that the tutor on duty is an expert on Management English and conclude that asking her would be the most efficient and logical way of dealing with the problem in the situation.

If he did all of this, it could be said that Mario has an understanding of the alternatives available to him, assessing each in the light of his need and the constraints of the context, and selecting his problem-solving strategy. In other words, he has been making informed decisions about his learning. He has been using his capacity for autonomy. But the tutor cannot see this process, only the outcome. Is it, then, fair or useful to assess the development of learner autonomy on the basis of observable behaviour? I would suggest not – and this is the real crux of the problem in evaluating autonomy.

To summarise, autonomy in language learning is generally accepted to be a psychological construct of capacity. In looking for evidence that learners exhibit increasing degrees of autonomy during a programme of learning, it is necessary to find ways in which the development of this capacity can be monitored.

Evaluating capacity

The measurement of proficiency gains, feedback from teachers and learners and an understanding of the learning context are important elements in the evaluation of autonomy in language learners. However, the principal challenge is to evaluate the 'capacity' for making informed decisions about language learning. In other words, it is necessary to monitor learners' metacognitive awareness, an area which has mostly been neglected by the teaching profession and educational researchers.

Metacognitive awareness

The term 'metacognition' was first used by Flavell (1970), and refers to the learners' awareness of the learning processes. Metacognitive strategies, for example, are those which involve learners in thinking about their learning, and include planning learning, organising resources, self-assessment and monitoring progress. They contribute strongly to learning success: 'Students without metacognitive approaches are essentially learners without direction and ability to review their progress, accomplishments and future learning directions' (O'Malley *et al.*, 1985a:24).

The link between the development of metacognitive awareness and learner autonomy is clear; current definitions of autonomy in language learning assume that learners have the capacity to make informed decisions about their learning. In other words, they *know* about learning. This means that the development of metacognition through learner training is crucial and its evaluation central to the search for proof of the efficacy of promoting autonomy. This capacity for making informed decisions about learning involves developing in the learner a deeper metacognitive awareness of at least three important areas:

- the learner him/herself as a learner
- the subject matter, i.e. in this case, the English language
- the processes of learning.

These can be elaborated as follows:

Self	attitudes
	beliefs
	expectations
	motivation
	needs
	learning style
	preferred learning environment
The English language	language awareness
	systems
	varieties
	similarities and differences between mother tongue and target language
	social appropriacy
	cultural appropriacy
	pragmatics
Learning process	activity evaluation
	strategy evaluation
	self-assessment
	goal-setting
	monitoring
	organising

Figure 1   Aspects of metacognitive awareness

A positive link between metacognitive awareness and success in language learning (one of the aims of promoting autonomy) is supported by research reported by Jones et al. in 1987, who studied the differences between effective and ineffective learners in terms of awareness of different types of strategies. They found that effective learners were aware of the processes underlying their own learning processes and attempted to use appropriate strategies to manage their own learning. Nunan (1997:57), reporting on earlier work (1991), found that one of the characteristics of successful language learners was 'the ability to reflect on and articulate processes underlying their own learning.'

Possible criteria for assessing metacognitive awareness

The writer's research in progress with learners of English at Temasek Polytechnic in Singapore has suggested a number of questions which may constitute useful criteria for assessing levels of metacognitive awareness in learners, and, thus, the development of a capacity for autonomy. (See Figure 2.)

Can students:

- provide a rationale for their choice of learning activities and materials?
- describe the strategies they used?
- provide an evaluation of the strategies used?
- identify their strengths and weaknesses?
- describe their plans for learning?
- describe alternative strategies that they could have used?

Figure 2   Criteria for assessing metacognitive awareness

Questions deriving from the criteria can be put to learners by teachers when discussing their work with them and typically focus on 'what?', 'how?' and 'why?' For example:

- Why did you do this piece of work?
- Why did you choose this particular text/activity?
- Did you like it? Why? Why not?
- How did you go about doing this activity?
- Why did you do it in this way?
- How well did you do?
- What, if any, problems did you have?
- Why did you have them?
- What did you do about them? Why?
- What is your plan for next week? Why?
- How will you do it? Why?

Such questions are, of course, familiar to learner trainers and are nothing new in themselves, but, in order to be useful for evaluation purposes, they would need to be asked systematically and consistently. The extent to which the students are able to respond to such questions will provide clues as to their levels of metacognitive awareness. One question, in particular, is very useful since it requires of the learners a high degree of learning awareness in order to answer it: *What else could you have done/could you do?*

Suggestions for evaluating the responses

Learners' responses to such questions or prompts would need to be categorised according to the levels of awareness they showed. To develop a framework for the latter may be no simple matter and the results of current research into examples of appropriate scales and criteria are awaited. Preliminary data from Singapore, however, suggests that it might be useful to consider three levels or stages of metacognitive awareness, as evidenced by both the type of language used by learners in their responses to prompts and by their content (See Figure 3 below.):

- level 1: largely unaware
- level 2: becoming aware (the transition stage)
- level 3: largely aware.

Level of awareness	Language characterised by	Typical examples
Level 1 largely unaware	• description with little or no rationale • formulaic or 'shallow' rationales • broad statements with little or no support • few or naive questions • little or incorrect use of metalanguage	'I read the text then I answered the questions.' 'I need English to get a good job.' 'English grammar is very difficult.'
Level 2 becoming aware (transition stage)	**greater** use of: • anecdotal evidence • introspection (expression of thoughts/feelings) • metaphor • 'epiphanies' • questions • metalanguage	'Yes, I've had problems with that...I made a big mistake...I was at my friend's house for party ... er birthday party ... and a woman...' 'I feel...', 'I think...', 'I've noticed that...' 'I felt...' 'I thought...', 'I noticed that...' 'Learning phrasal verbs is like wrestling with a jelly!' 'I've just realised that this strategy – the one I've always used – doesn't work for me very well.' 'If my intonation is wrong, how will it affect the person who is listening?'
Level 3 largely aware	**Confident and competent** use of the above *plus*: • descriptions of alternative strategies	'I could have learnt these words by writing them down with translations or by recording them on to a cassette listening, but I decided to use a word-web because I find I can remember the words more easily when I do this.'

Figure 3 Evaluating linguistic evidence of metacognitive awareness in language learners

Learners who are exhibiting metacognitive awareness will tend to use more personal language, including anecdotes and metaphors to describe their experiences of and feelings about learning. It has been suggested that the use of anecdote by a learner demonstrates that he/she has reflected on the experience, considers it significant and has taken pains to formulate the 'story' in such a way as to be relevant to the topic being discussed (Jarvis 1996). The use of metaphor can indicate even greater reflective depth and reveal much about a learner's own insights into learning (c.f. 'wrestling with a jelly', in Figure 3 above). Those learners who consistently and competently make use of the linguistic features described in stage two but who, in addition, are able to demonstrate awareness of alternative strategies or approaches to the learning task or problem could be regarded as having reached stage three of metacognitive awareness and, therefore, largely aware of the learning processes as they pertain to themselves and their own learning.

Further research is required in order to confirm that such a hierarchy is truly representative of the stages of the development of metacognitive awareness, but it is suggested that such a framework may be a useful starting point for experiments.

Practical techniques for eliciting metacognitive awareness

There are a number of techniques the teacher can employ in order to prompt learners to provide evidence of metacognitive awareness. For example, the teacher may introduce regular 'learning conversations' (Harri-Augstein and Thomas, 1991; Kelly, 1996). This is a technique which is becoming common practice in self-access learning contexts where learning support is provided for students. Generally, learning conversations aim to help learners become more aware of the learning process as it relates to them personally and to enable learners to articulate experiences of ideas, insights and feelings about learning. They may be viewed as constituting learners' training in developing metacognitive awareness.

An example of where this is used is the Centre for Individual Language Learning (CILL) at Temasek Polytechnic in Singapore, where a new Certificate in Independent Learning is being introduced which actively requires the assessment of the development of autonomy in the learners (Ravindran, 1998). In CILL, learners undergo a course of learner training and then carry out a number of learning projects on their own. In a final learning conversation, the learner presents evidence of learning to a consultant in the form of a portfolio. In such a context, it would be possible for the consultant and the learner to discuss items in the portfolio, with the consultant using appropriate prompts in order to elicit responses from the learner which could then be assessed using the three stages of awareness presented above.

An alternative or supplementary way of encouraging learners to consider such prompts would be to ask them to write a commentary on their learning, perhaps in the form of a diary or journal, or as a 'letter' to their consultant/teacher. Diaries and journals can be useful, but often their content is too broad and unfocused; learners are not always aware of the purpose of a journal.

Journals are not normally used for evaluation purposes and to do so requires a different approach. Teachers would need to provide a careful guide as to what kind of revelations are encouraged. 'Letters' or reports to the consultant or teacher may be easier to manage in this respect. A framework of appropriate questions can be provided for the learners to write on. Knowing the audience and the purpose of the writing may well encourage the learners to write in a more focused and detailed way in order to 'show off' their insights into their learning. Another idea would be make a list of suitable questions part of specific learning tasks so that learners are encouraged to become used to reflecting on their learning in this way.

Some constraints
Language proficiency
One constraint that both the teacher and researcher face when attempting to evaluate metacognitive awareness in the ways described above is the learners' levels of language proficiency. Is it unrealistic to expect learners to speak revealingly of their knowledge about language learning in the target language? Should such activities be undertaken in the mother tongue? Encouraging learners to use their mother tongue to talk about language learning would provide much richer data for the researcher, assuming that he/she can use the mother tongue too, or can obtain accurate translations, and may also be a more feasible way for teachers of the same linguistic background as their learners to go about such evaluation. This may not always be possible, however, and teachers will need to be aware that, if the learners are operating in the target language, it would be unrealistic to expect highly detailed insights. Such learners will need, of course, learner training in order to become familiar with such reflective activities and will need to be taught the necessary language and metalanguage to support this. (The research currently in progress in Singapore is investigating the differences in student responses when the learning conversation partner is a Singaporean and when it is a non-Singaporean, i.e. the researcher. It will be interesting to see whether responses in a Singaporean variety of English (e.g.'Singlish') will be more revealing than those in a more standard variety of English.)

Age and maturity of students
Many teachers may feel that the approaches outlined in this paper are not applicable to younger learners, who may not be mature enough to talk about their learning in a revealing manner. It may be that such learning conversations, for example, are more suited to older learners, but it has been demonstrated convincingly that even very young learners are able to talk about their learning in a meaningful way which develops in them greater metacognitive awareness. Younger learners may, however, need different kinds of prompts and a teacher who is prepared to the take time to probe their responses. For further information on developing metacognition in young learners, see Ellis (this volume).

Time

Another constraint is the amount of time that the evaluation of learners' metacognitive awareness entails; there are implications for the staffing and the management of the autonomous or self-access learning, as well as for the physical resources required, such as space for counselling sessions. Specific learning materials and instruments may need to be designed. In other words, just as an investment in autonomy means a financial investment by an institution in staffing, facilities and resources, so does a commitment to evaluating autonomy.

Conclusion

From the definition of autonomy presented earlier it is apparent that learner autonomy is not an easily described single behaviour. Furthermore, there are so many variables which affect a learner's degree of autonomy at any one time that it is clearly impossible to evaluate autonomy based on observable behaviour. It has been suggested that in the evaluation of autonomy in learners it is important to collect evidence of learners' proficiency gains, as well as to consider feedback from them and their teachers.

It has also been suggested that evaluating the development of metacognitive awareness in learners is central to any evaluation of autonomy and that this would necessitate the development of appropriate criteria and scales for categorising learners' self-report data. Research is needed to identify correlations between these different aspects of evaluating autonomy, and to provide a practical framework that can be used by teachers and learners in the learning context. If we are not mindful of these gaps in our knowledge, the language teaching profession will be able to justify the promotion of learner autonomy only as an 'act of faith'.

9 Developing Children's Metacognitive Awareness

Gail Ellis
British Council, Paris

Metacognitive awareness, the knowledge and self-awareness a learner has about their own learning process, is regarded as the key to successful language learning. However, it is often thought that children are too young to possess this awareness, but research has shown that even quite young children do show a considerable degree of metacognitive knowledge and that this can be developed. Classroom experience has also shown that, asked the right questions and given the opportunity, children not only possess an awareness about their own learning which they are often not given credit for, but this awareness can indeed be developed to enable children to express themselves in a purposeful and meaningful way. Why do classroom situations and most teaching materials rarely address this crucial aspect of learning in any explicit or systematic way? What are the right questions to ask and how can this awareness be developed? What are the benefits of developing metacognitive awareness in terms of performance – linguistic outcomes and perceiving progress; affective outcomes – developing motivation and positive attitudes towards language learning, the foreign language and culture; and behavioural outcomes – developing a more serious and co-operative approach to learning? This paper will attempt to answer these questions and offer a methodology which can be integrated into current teaching practices for young learners.

What is metacognitive awareness?

There has been much debate over a suitable definition (see Sinclair, this volume). Brown (1978) defines it as 'knowing about knowing'. In a language learning context this means knowing about oneself as a learner, in other words, the knowledge and self-awareness a learner has of their own language learning process.

Metacognition and children

What about metacognition and children? Quite young children possess a considerable degree of metacognitive knowledge. I asked my five-year-old daughter on a visit to the countryside in spring how she remembered the names of the wild flowers we saw:

> Mother *How do you remember the names of the flowers?*
> Child *I think in my head.*
> Mother *What do you think?*
> Child *I think of the flowers.*
> Mother *What do you think about the flowers? For example, what's different about them?*
> Child *The colour.*
> Mother *Yes, so can you remember the names of two flowers we saw that are the same colour?*
> Child *Periwinkle and violet.*
> Mother *That's right. What colour are they?*
> Child *Purple.*
> Mother *Yes. But they are not the same are they? How do you know which is the periwinkle and which is the violet? What's different about them? Do you remember when we looked at them carefully?*
> Child *The size.*
> Mother *Which flower is bigger? The periwinkle or the violet?*
> Child *The periwinkle...*

The interaction between mother and daughter that takes place during this extract shows that through a series of probing oral questions which required the child to introspect, she was led to a conscious statement of the strategies she used to recall the names of the flowers. It can be assumed that this questioning process enabled the child to become aware of the strategies she used. In addition, it seems that this process was an enjoyable experience, proved by the fact that the child requested to speak about the same subject the next day.

However, it is often thought that children are not capable of expressing their opinions or views about how they learn, of understanding the strategies they use, or of understanding instructions or explanations about learning. The following quote reflects the resistance many teachers show when asked to address this crucial aspect of learning: 'To tell a classroom of eight-year-olds what the aims of a lesson are, is, in my opinion, pointless'. Consequently, most teaching situations and many teaching materials do not contribute to the development of metacognitive awareness. However, it is generally agreed that the learning purposes, strategies and the possibility of strategy transfer to other tasks must, at some point in the learning process, be made explicit to the learner. It is, therefore, the responsibility of the concerned, individual teacher to add this missing dimension.

This can be done in a variety of ways: through information given by the teacher or materials, by guided questioning or through learner discussion. The learners should not be left to uncover the implicit without some kind of prompt or help. This is especially important with young learners who have not yet acquired the expertise and experience of older learners who may be able to work out the aims of a lesson for themselves if their teacher or materials do not state what they are explicitly. There is also the view that explicit raising to consciousness of the processes of learning can occur through learner interaction and does not necessarily need direct intervention. Whatever our view, we can at least agree that, in some way, learners need to become consciously aware of what they are doing and why and how this can help them in future learning.

My own classroom practice has shown that children are capable of understanding and benefit from being given information about classroom procedures. Furthermore, asked the right questions, they are capable of expressing an awareness about their own learning that they are rarely given credit for, and this awareness can be developed. The kind of awareness or knowledge that children do have about their learning is the comparative difficulty of different types of tasks, knowledge about themselves as learners and of the ways in which they generally operate strategically. What does not develop either as fast or as inevitably is the ability to use that knowledge spontaneously in pursuance of a cognitive goal. As Brown (1978) says 'Young children can do much more than they will do'. A reality we are all well aware of.

Metacognitive awareness in a language learning context

In a language learning context with young learners I see metacognitive awareness as an umbrella term (Figure 1) which incorporates the following areas. These overlap to some extent and all involve the development of positive attitudes.

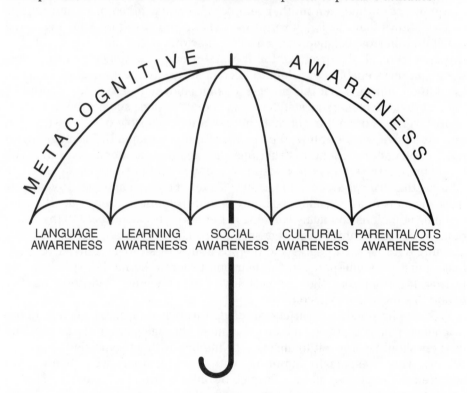

Figure 1 Metacognitive awareness is an umbrella term

Language awareness

The aim here is to stimulate children's interest and curiosity about language 'to challenge pupils to ask questions about language' (Hawkins, 1984) in order to develop understanding of and knowledge about language in general, including the foreign language, the mother tongue and, if appropriate and depending on the context, other languages. This would involve using metalanguage (the mother tongue or target language) for stating the aims of a lesson, for explaining the use of different classroom activities, for signposting the different stages of a lesson, for giving classroom instructions, for describing language, for analysing language, for making comparisons to find similarities and differences between the L1 and L2, for discovering rules and for developing positive attitudes towards the foreign language and language learning.

Learning/cognitive awareness

The main aim here is to help children understand why they are learning a foreign language at school, and that in addition to linguistic outcomes, it also offers important personal, cognitive, cultural, affective and social gains. It involves explaining to children how they are going to learn a foreign language in class, the type of materials they are going to use and the activities they are going to do; getting them to think about how they learn, which strategies they use to help them to remember, to concentrate, to pay attention; how and when to review, how to monitor their learning and decide what they need to do next; how to build their confidence and give them the language which will empower them to take control of their learning when, for example, they don't understand, to enable them to become more responsible and independent in the learning process, as well as creating positive attitudes to language learning.

Social awareness

This area of language learning can be related to Vygotsky's (1978) sociocultural theory of learning: that higher cognitive functions are internalised from social interaction. This will involve children in collaborative activities which, in many contexts, will involve a new understanding of how to behave in class, towards the teacher and towards each other; to establish a working consensus which will contribute towards building class, peer, teacher and individual respect; and to learn to interact and co-operate together in activities and to develop positive attitudes to sharing and working together in class.

Cultural awareness

Girard's (in Brewster *et al.* 1991:33) definition of this important area 'to develop understanding and openness towards others' would involve children in activities which would enable them to discover similarities and differences between themselves and other people and to see these in a positive light. The development of tolerance and positive attitudes to the foreign language culture and people will draw children away from a mono-cultural perspective and into a broader view of the world.

Parental and other teaching staff awareness

The introduction of foreign language learning and its accompanying methodologies into an existing primary system, may have great reverberations
throughout the school. Such learning may be perceived by children, other
teaching staff and parents as 'less formal', 'not serious enough', 'less disciplined'
and its value may be questioned. The changes required by the introduction of
foreign language teaching methodologies can cause animosity between other
teaching staff, distrust by parents and confusion and misbehaviour of the children. As Binns (1998) points out 'One has to be aware of the difficulties that
may arise from a different style of teaching, and realise that other people may
require time and explanations of what you are doing and why'. People need
time to adjust to new systems and they need to understand what the aims of
foreign language teaching are and how they are to be achieved. In this sense, it
is very important that other teaching staff, parents and, of course, the children
themselves, receive 'methodological preparation' as defined by Dickinson and
Carver (1980) so they are informed about methodological approaches and materials in order to understand what is going on in the classroom and why. This
aspect will be discussed further in metacognition, classroom management and
lesson planning below.

Why is the development of metacognitive awareness important?

As already stated, the development of metacognitive awareness is considered
to be the key to successful learning.

Children get lots of implicit practice in the classroom in experimenting with
different cognitive strategies, for example tasks that get them to sort or clas-
sify, to compare, to match, to select, to predict, to guess, to sequence, etc., but
most classroom situations and materials rarely inform children explicitly about
why they are using certain strategies or get them to reflect on how they are
learning. In other words, the metacognitive dimension is missing, so children
are not helped to understand the significance of what they are doing. Although
some published materials now include activities which get children to review
what they have learnt (see Sinclair and Ellis, 1992), these are in the form of self-
tests or checklists which focus solely on the product or the linguistic content of
a learning unit and not, in any way, on the processes involved. The emphasis
here is 'on learning something rather than on learning to learn' (Wenden and
Rubin, 1987). The inclusion of simple instruments for self-assessment is also a
welcome addition to published materials, but again these rarely encourage any
reflection on the learning process and simply involve children in mechanical
acts of drawing or sticking a smiling face if they liked a unit or an unsmiling
face if they didn't, with no consideration of the reasons why. The accompanying
teachers' notes rarely suggest or offer guidance on the questions they can ask
to get children to think about and justify the reasons for their choice, which
would lead them to a greater understanding of themselves as learners.

Pupils need activities which incorporate: *reflection*, thinking about what they
are going to do and why; *experimentation*, doing a task and manipulating the
language to achieve a goal such as listen and colour, listen and draw, listen and

sequence; and *further reflection*: What did I do?' Why did I do it? How did I do it? How well did I do? What do I need to do next? In this way, the implicit becomes explicit – pupils become aware of what they are doing and why. We can assume that 'the more informed (and aware) children/learners are about language and language learning the more effective they will be at managing their own learning and at language learning' (Ellis and Sinclair, 1989).

A methodology for developing metacognitive awareness

A methodology for developing metacognitive awareness could be applied to existing classroom contexts with little disruption. Most lessons consist, more or less, of three principal stages: revision and presentation of language items and planning and preparation for an activity; doing an activity or a task to practise the language items and to develop skills areas; further practise to consolidate, extend and review the language practised, perhaps in a different context and/or to produce an outcome such as a book, a poster, a completed worksheet and so on. Applied to the skills areas, for example, listening, these stages are usually referred to as pre-, while- and post-listening. These stages provide the teacher with a framework in which to incorporate *reflection, experimentation* and *further reflection* as mentioned above representing the on-going cyclical nature of learning in which children *plan, do* and *review* (Figure 2). This general strategy for learning is important because it can be used as a framework for learning any subject, including language learning.

STAGE 1 ⟫ STAGE 2 ⟫ STAGE 3

PRE-LISTENING ⟫ WHILE-LISTENING ⟫ POST-LISTENING

REFLECTION ⟫ EXPERIMENTATION ⟫ FURTHER REFLECTION

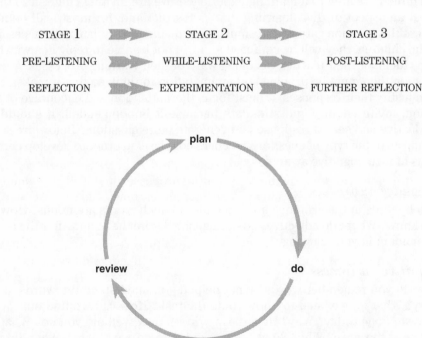

Figure 2   A methodology for developing metacognitive awareness

In order to do this teachers will need to expand their role (Wenden, 1985) by taking on a guiding, questioning role which will involve informing children about language learning and what they are doing and how they are going to do it. They can do this by prompting, modelling questions and strategies, demonstrating, discussing learning and helping children reflect on what they have done, how they did it and how well they did. This is an approach I have used regularly with children in France. Working in this way with beginner or low level learners naturally requires the use of the mother tongue and a little extra time. The extra time can easily be found if the teacher is prepared to take a few minutes away from the content of the foreign language lesson to focus on the process. Getting children to focus on the process of what they do will be a new experience for most. At first their replies to questions will be vague and they will need to be pushed to think and justify their responses. Such an approach needs to be built up gradually over a period of time but, little by little, children become more aware of the foreign language learning process and of themselves as language learners, more efficient at thinking for themselves and much more actively and personally involved in their own learning.

Asking the right questions

Reference has been made to the teacher's expanded role which includes taking on a questioning role. What are the right questions to ask to encourage active reflection? The questions we ask children about their learning have to be clear and directly related to a learning experience. We are inviting children to think about an aspect of their learning that is abstract and, for most, will be new. Unless the questions are well formulated and concrete, in language accessible to the children, they will be confused and will not be able to reply in a way that helps them, or their teacher, become aware of their learning processes. A good question then must be probing and an invitation to think so that it makes children justify their responses, it must focus their attention and encourage observation, invite enquiry and stimulate because it is open-ended. It should be productive and seek a response and generate more questions. Below are some examples of the type of questions teachers could ask in order to develop certain areas of metacognitive awareness:

Language awareness

Which words in the sentence are adjectives? Which words are nouns? How do you know? Where do adjectives go in English? Before the noun? After the noun? What about in your language?

Cognitive awareness

How do you remember words? What helped you understand the words in the story? What do we need to know to do the task? How can we find out? What have we done today? Why? How did we do it? How well did you do? What do you need to revise? Why? What are you going to do next? Why? What did you do if you didn't understand? How did you check your work? How did you work out the answers?

Cultural awareness
What can you see in the picture? What's the same as in (France)? What's different? Can you explain? Why?

Metacognition, classroom management and lesson planning

Many day-to-day problems teachers encounter are related to aspects of class-room management and lesson planning. The following list was drawn up by a group of teachers in Turkey who have recently introduced English into their primary curriculum:

- Pupils' attitude towards English as a subject is not serious enough. There is too big a difference between the way English is taught at school and the other subjects.
- Pupils are often irresponsible, noisy and careless.
- Pupils often show little respect to their peers or their teacher.
- Children learn quickly but forget quickly.
- Pupils are often undisciplined.
- Pupils often have little concept of limits or restrictions in the classroom.
- It is often difficult to maintain children's concentration and attention.
- Class sizes are often large and difficult to organise.
- Mixed ability classes and mixed behaviour are difficult to manage.
- Pupils rarely listen to each other or their teacher.

As can be seen, many of the problems listed above relate to the five areas of metacognitive awareness defined above, so by developing these, many of the problems could be overcome by:

- providing methodological preparation for children, other teaching staff and parents
- planning lessons that incorporate good staging, timing and pace, and sign-posting
- giving clear instructions and demonstrations
- maintaining class cohesion and attention to maintain children's interest and to avoid boredom
- using activities that challenge children and make them think
- involving all children and providing variety
- equipping children with the strategies and language for coping with situations where they do not have the appropriate language, so they can nevertheless participate and avoid communication breakdowns and maintain the tempo of the lesson
- building in opportunities for recapping, revising and reviewing
- having strategies for controlling children and building up class respect.

A lack of these result in a loss of concentration and boredom of the children and a loss of control on behalf of the teacher. There is a close link, therefore, between good classroom management skills and lesson planning and the development of metacognitive awareness.

Methodological preparation

In terms of classroom management and control, the teacher needs to be explicit about what is going on in the classroom and why. As already mentioned, the methodological approaches to teaching English may contrast starkly to the way other subjects are taught at primary school, and children may not understand the teacher's reasons for using activities such as songs, games, pair work, stories, role plays and may regard them as 'not serious' and an opportunity to relax and have some fun. Teachers should tell their pupils why they are using such activities so they understand the pedagogical implications and learning benefits:

> *We use songs because they help you memorise the language and learn the*
> *pronunciation and rhythm of English.*
> *We use games because they get you to use language in a real way.*
> *We ask you to speak to each other in English so everyone gets lots of practice.*
> *We use stories because they help you learn to listen and understand the general*
> *meaning. It doesn't matter if you don't understand every word.*

Lesson planning

It can be seen that the *plan do review* strategy can be applied to the general structure of a lesson. Teachers need to reflect on their lesson structure in terms of the learning process as well as the product, and on how they can explain to the children in an explicit and accessible way what the aims of a lesson are, and how they are going to be achieved. It should be clear to children how the lesson progresses from one stage to the next gradually working towards the stated goal. It may be possible to involve children in the actual planning of the lesson, although in most contexts this would probably prove difficult because of constraints of time, but there is no reason why pupils should not be asked to think about what the planning or preparation for a learning opportunity were post-event. See, for example, some sample lesson plans incorporating such an approach (Ellis and Brewster, 1991; Brewster, Ellis and Girard, 1991).

Stating the aims of a lesson

As mentioned above it is important to state the aims of a lesson or activity so children see its relevance:

> *Today we are going to listen to a story about a dog called Spot. Where's Spot?*
> *Is he behind, under or on the table?*
> *Now we are going to play a game to practise the prepositions.*

This type of explanation should help children to become more aware of what they are learning and why and to understand why their English class may seem different to their other classes.

Signposting

It is important that children understand how their lesson progresses from one stage to the next so they can understand how they are going to achieve the stated aims. Clear signposting helps children perceive what they are doing and where they are going. Teachers need to give clear and explicit signposts in their lesson:

> *First, we are going to revise 'x' from our last lesson. What do you remember?*
> *What did we learn? How did we do it?*
> *Now we are going to learn some new words/prepositions/a new structure.*
> *Listen carefully!*
> *Now we are going to play a game to practise the words/prepositions/structure.*
> *Let's review/revise.*
> *How did you do? Why?*

In this way, pupils can perceive how they move from one stage of a lesson in the pursuit of a goal. Such signposts may initially need to be given in the native language but, little by little, pupils will acquire this metalanguage in English and less and less native language will need to be used.

Reviewing

Teachers also need to plan opportunities for recapping, revising and reviewing not just at the end of a lesson but also throughout as children constantly need to recycle what they have learned so they don't forget. If reviewing is built into classes on a systematic basis this will help pupils understand what they have been learning and perceive their progress and maintain motivation.

Applying the *plan do review* strategy

It is the responsibility of the teacher to create a context and purpose for learning, and I would like to describe a learning opportunity that I was able to exploit and to which I attempted to apply the *plan do review* strategy to develop children's metacognitive awareness. It involved a class of nine- and ten-year-olds from a state primary school in Paris, and Britain's Prime Minister, Tony Blair, who came to Paris and, as part of his visit, included a session with children in the British Council's Young Learners Centre. In view of the children's limited English, it was decided that this should take the form of a question/answer session as this would provide a situation which could be child-led in order to ensure some degree of linguistic control.

This context provided an ideal opportunity for the children to review, practise and expand question forms they had learned during the year, as well as an opportunity to discover cultural information and to make cultural comparisons.

Planning/preparation stage

Basing our work on question forms, the children decided which questions they would ask a VIP such as Jacques Chirac, the Queen or Tony Blair and the necessary vocabulary was introduced, revised and practised. Classroom activities involved practice of the question forms in class repetition and choral drilling, pair work and role plays. When the important day arrived, the children were well prepared to use and experiment with their questions in an authentic situation where there was a genuine information gap.

An extract from the question/answer session is given below.

> Pupil *Do you like tea?*
> TB *Do I like tea? Yes. All English people like tea. It's obligatoire!*
> Pupil *Have you got a pet?*
> TB *Have I got a pet? Er, well. We have a .... in the house that we live ... er ... we had a cat but we are getting a new cat.*
> Pupil *Do you like chocolate?*
> TB *Chocolate? I'm afraid so. I like it too much. And my wife likes it very, very much.*
> Pupil *Can you speak French?*
> TB *Un petit peu.*
> Pupil *Can you cook?*
> TB *Er ... I cook like I play the guitar. I cook badly. But I can cook. I cook for my children sometimes but they complain!*

The interaction was limited and the unpredictable and expanded replies were often beyond the comprehension of the pupils. However, they were not flummoxed and there were no communication breakdowns. Most significantly, it provided an opportunity for the pupils to use the target language beyond the walls of their familiar classroom, a memorable and genuine context in which to use English. The session was entirely child-led. The children decided themselves which questions they were going to ask, no-one asked the same question twice which proved they were listening attentively, and it provided plenty of comprehensible input.

Review/follow-up stage

This consisted of four activities:
- to complete a souvenir worksheet to focus pupils' attention on the linguistic content of this learning opportunity by getting them to record their questions and Tony Blair's replies.
- to complete a questionnaire to focus pupils' attention on the processes involved throughout this learning opportunity, what they did before the question/answer session, what they did after and to evaluate their performance.
- to write a *thank-you* letter to Tony Blair.
- to view the video recording of the session and review the questions and replies and to evaluate their performance.

The souvenir worksheet was completed in a follow-up lesson. Together, the class recalled the questions they asked Tony Blair and his replies and recorded them on the worksheet. Working in this way as a whole class, meant that the children supported each other through their respective zones of proximal development (Vygotsky, 1978) and collaboratively completed the task by reviewing the linguistic content of the session. A video recording of the session, available at a later date, was used in a similar way to review linguistic content. Finally, the children evaluated their performance. They were delighted and proud of their performance – an opinion fully supported by their teachers.

The questionnaire provided the metacognitive dimension by encouraging children to reflect on the processes involved before and after the session and to evaluate their performance. Below, translated from French, are some of their comments.

Before the visit
What did we do in class to prepare the visit?

> *We asked lots of questions and we revised.*
> *We were asked lots of questions.*
> *We practised asking our neighbours lots of questions.*

After the visit
How well did I do?

Asking questions: All children gave themselves a good rating for the questions they asked justified by the following reasons:

> *Because he understood what we asked him.*
> *We weren't frightened, we were calm.*
> *Because I had worked hard and he understood very well.*

Understanding the replies: They gave themselves only a quite good or OK rating for understanding the replies for the following reasons:

> *Because he spoke too fast.*
> *Because he used words which we haven't learnt yet.*
> *We understood the beginning but not the end.*

The children were honest and frank with their assessment and their comments showed insight. They reflect an understanding of what they did well and what was more difficult and the reasons why. The following comments reveal the cultural and affective benefits gained from the session:

What did I learn?

> *I learnt how to speak to an important person.*
> *I learnt vocabulary and how to ask questions.*
> *I learnt a lot about the English language and culture.*

What did I personally get out of this visit?

> *I was very happy and proud to have been able to speak to an important person.*
> *I found out what he liked and what he could do.*
> *It was very interesting and if I could do it again I would!*

The *plan do review* strategy to develop children's metacognitive awareness was applied to this learning opportunity in a way that did not disrupt classroom procedures or interfere with the syllabus. The extra time needed to complete the questionnaire was considered a necessary and worthwhile investment. It also allowed the type of questions that children will be able to ask themselves independently at a later stage to be modelled. But does developing children's metacognitive awareness make them better foreign language learners? This I cannot say as I have never had the opportunity to set up a controlled study and a great deal of research still needs to be done to find out the rate at which a learner gains more self-awareness of their own learning process (see Sinclair, this volume). What I do know and have observed is that children develop a greater understanding of themselves as language learners, become more actively and personally involved and develop strong motivation and positive attitudes towards language learning. These, as a preparation for more formal FLL in secondary school, I consider to be valuable and worthwhile outcomes.

My own work and observations have been reinforced by those of colleagues in Turkey also attempting to develop their pupils' metacognitive awareness:

> *At the beginning they weren't studying but now they are studying more seriously. I think they are enjoying English lessons now.*

> *They participate more, they ask more questions at the right time and to move on to the next stage in the course of an activity. They feel confident and happy.*

> *At the beginning they weren't very serious or they didn't follow the lessons seriously. They thought language learning only meant fun. Now they are a bit more serious, they are trying to use it. But some problem students are still a problem. They don't know how to listen to the others.*

To conclude, I would hope that the teaching profession will be able to move away from the attitude: 'To tell a classroom of eight-year-olds what the aims of a lesson are, is, in my opinion, pointless', to one where there is a recognition of the benefits of and a purposeful move towards the development of children's metacognitive awareness. This crucial aspect of learning can be integrated into the teacher's general day-to-day classroom procedures of classroom management and lesson planning.

Acknowledgements
The quotes from Turkish teachers come from teachers working at the Isik Schools of the Feyziye Schools Foundation, Istanbul.

10 What's On? Factors for Success in Learning English Online

Marti Sevier
British Council, Singapore

Introduction

The use of the Internet in education, for students of all ages, is a phenomenon whose impact we can hardly begin to measure. Across the world, children as young as five and six are being taught search skills on the Internet while their older siblings, parents and grandparents are enrolling in courses and even taking degrees online. In the field of English as a second/foreign language, online courses and resources for language learning are burgeoning to the extent that one researcher estimates that there are 'between one hundred and two hundred sites specifically devoted to language learning activities and materials' (Eastment, 1996). ESL/EFL teachers seem, in fact, to be among the strongest adherents of using the Internet: Galloway notes, for example, that the TESL-L listserv, which operates out of City University of New York, is 'the largest interactive list on the Internet' (Galloway, 1996:1).

In Singapore, both government and private schools, primary and secondary, as well as tertiary institutions have begun to explore and exploit the possibilities of learning English on the Internet.

Recently the British Council, Singapore has joined these institutions in offering an online writing course for Cambridge examination candidates utilising computer-mediated communication, or CMC. This paper will attempt to address issues related to learning English online and discuss our experience in this area by considering the following questions:

- What advantages does course delivery on the Internet offer to learners, specifically English language learners?
- What factors impede success in online learning?
- What are essential online learning skills and learning characteristics?
- How do students enrolled in online English language courses view these questions?

In considering these questions I hope to answer a fifth question:

- What recommendations can be made to ensure success in teaching and learning online?

What advantages does course delivery on the Internet offer to learners, specifically English language learners?

Many of the advantages of learning on the Internet are related to the issues of learner control.

One feature is *asynchronicity*: learners and teachers can log on at any time of the day or night and are thus able to 'fit in' teaching and learning when it is convenient to them.

Asynchronicity can enable learning to become *place-independent*, assuming the learner has access to a computer at home or elsewhere. Since the learner need not be tied to a particular location, online education can provide a unique service to those who cannot leave home for any reason.

A third feature of CMC is that it ensures learner *anonymity*. For many learners this is highly liberating, enabling them to transcend perceptions of status and social position by working online from the privacy of their terminals. Often those who would not ordinarily participate in a face-to-face discussion feel freer to 'speak out' online. Contributions of course participants may be highly valued, perhaps more so than those from the course tutor. There is a loss of teacher authority and gain in learner autonomy.

A fourth feature of online education is its *ability to support a wide range of pedagogical techniques*, which can in turn support a wide range of individual learning styles. Paulsen (1995) lists a range of techniques in terms of their interaction pattern and the type of online resources utilised, including:

- *one-alone techniques*, which can be performed by the learner without intervention and include various forms of information retrieval, such as conducting searches on the Internet;
- *one-to-one techniques*, which include learning contracts, apprenticeships, internships, and other forms of correspondence study; usually this is between the learner and the lecturer and often utilises e-mail;
- *one-to-many techniques*, which may take the form of lectures, symposia, skits, or even a set of directions from the facilitator or group leader on how a task is to be completed, and;
- *many-to-many techniques*, used with conferencing software; these may include debates, simulations, or games. Role plays, case studies, discussion groups and transcript-based assignments are all now in use.

Fifthly, CMC is also seen as a means of *supporting global education*, wherein learners of all ages and all nationalities 'meet' and interact with others 'across time zones and across cultures' (Wells, 1995). Learners in our Singapore centre are able to interact with their counterparts from other English Language Centres in the British Council network.

Although there are conflicting views regarding the effectiveness of online learning, certainly a sixth feature of CMC is that it can *replicate many of the attributes of face-to-face learning*, a point corroborated in Paulsen's list above.

Information and ideas can be shared and some claim that the learning which takes place is 'deeper' than that which takes place in an ordinary classroom:

The nature of the on-line domain contributes to enabling and supporting active learning. Students actively present ideas and respond to one another's formulations, a process which contributes to facilitating higher developmental levels of understanding. The acts of formulating and verbalising one's own ideas as well as responding to ideas by one's peers are important cognitive skills. Active participation also creates a particularly information-rich environment, providing each student with multiple perspectives on an idea or theme (Harasim, 1989:54).

Hiltz (1995:3) also reports an 'improved ability [on the part of learners] to apply the material of the course in new contexts and express their own independent ideas relating to the material'.These general claims also apply specifically to English language teaching and learning. Holliday (1997) claims the more specific gain of increased grammatical accuracy on the part of ESL and EFL learners through the use of e-mail. Leppänen and Kalaja (1995:35) report that the use of computer conferencing with EAP students in Finland gave students the opportunity to 'assume more roles' with less teacher feedback and greater awareness of themselves as members of a group.

However, while such claims are encouraging, it is necessary to keep in mind that the medium of CMC requires special strengths and skills, both on the part of the student and the teacher and also in course design. This brings us to our second question.

What factors impede success in online learning?

Many of the factors which impede success can be seen as social. Any form of online learning is a form of distance learning, so the issue of *transactional distance*, defined as 'a distance of understandings and perceptions caused in part by the geographic distance' should not be ignored, since it can lead to 'a psychological and communications gap, a space of potential misunderstanding between the inputs of instructor and those of the learner' (Moore, 1991).

One problem, then, is that of *isolation*. Although anonymity is viewed as an advantage, it can also be, for some learners, lonely and boring. Those accustomed to face-to-face communication in the classroom may find it difficult to 'read' the teacher or classmates solely on the basis of written messages and the occasional emoticon. Thus learners may encounter problems in adjusting their messages to relatively anonymous interlocutors, especially those from other cultures or academic communities.

CMC is at present primarily a *text-based medium*, and this brings a complex of problems. As Berge and Collins point out:

> Facility in writing is essential across the entire curriculum, and with the present technology one cannot communicate on a computer network without writing ... we must recognise that not all students can express themselves well in writing and, even for those who can, [...] writing and using online text-based applications can be a time-consuming struggle (Berge and Collins, 1995:6).

The online learner needs to learn and adjust to a *new style of writing*, especially in discussion tasks. This style is much like letter writing but different from the formal essay or report often done for mainstream, face-to-face courses. Furthermore, learners need to respond appropriately and succinctly to postings, which requires a knowledge of audience and an ability to analyse and summarise. Threading, an important aspect of CMC participation, presents further problems; a student may wish to make a comment that draws together two or more threads of a discussion and not know where to post it. This difficulty is exacerbated by poor software design which can result in discussion threads being difficult to follow or even find.

An online environment enables a transcript of all postings to be kept, which causes, for some, an element of *anxiety* in posting messages at all: a spoken miscue in a classroom is quickly forgotten, but in a 'permanent' medium like writing, one's flaws, perceived or real, become indelible. Although CMC is said to enable learners to transcend perceptions of status and social position, Grint points out that many learners in a study he conducted 'seemed to have adopted systems for reconstructing statuses. These included searching out personal résumés to confirm assumed status, and systematically ignoring those participants whose comments were considered trivial' (Grint, 1989:190). This could further increase anxiety on the part of the student who feels that s/he is not an expert in the group.

In an online environment, *asynchronicity*, often an advantage, can lead to problems. If we post a message to a conference, it is immediately available to other learners on a course. If no one responds, one may feel that one's contribution is worthless. Similarly, if an instructor does not respond quickly to a question, confusion and frustration can result. Learners must also respond quickly to postings: although working offline enables one to work at one's own pace to produce an articulate response, it is also true that these thoughts, or very similar ones, may already have been posted (Pincas, 1997).

Time management can be problematic: the flexibility afforded by the online environment requires the learner to organise his/her own learning; for many, as Pincas (ibid.) indicates, this can be more difficult than simply showing up in class at the appointed times. Many online learners have cited this problem in a discussion of why they have 'dropped out' of online courses: once one falls too far behind in a conference, the temptation to simply read postings rather than respond to them is nearly overwhelming. This problem can be linked to a *perceived lack of structure* which some learners view as a problem in learning online: they simply are not sure of what they are expected to do.

Students may also encounter *information overload*; in addition to postings, there may be readings to download and respond to. The capacity of CMC to deliver huge chunks of text and references to websites can be exciting if one has time to read everything, but daunting if one does not. Many students do not read quickly and find it difficult to identify key issues in texts. These shortcomings will work against their success in online learning, as will the inability to prioritise and exercise critical skills necessary to decide whether a posting is essential or merely tangential to a discussion.

Affecting all of the above is the issue of *technology*. Without computer hardware and software, and technical support, learning online is impossible, and so the learner is at the mercy of his/her system and that of the institution conducting the course. Many students do not have access to up-to-date equip ment and find that the conferencing software causes their systems to crash. Lightning strikes, primitive telephone systems and erratic power supplies can further frustrate the efforts of learners and teachers. Students who have little experience with computers or keyboards will be further frustrated.

Equally pervasive is the issue of *language*: at present, since most online courses are conducted in English, non-native speakers of the language will almost certainly be disadvantaged. It is perhaps no wonder that CMC is often viewed as a very mixed blessing.

What are the characteristics and skills of successful online learners?

In order to answer this question, one can work backward from the points given above: at least some factors which impede success can be overcome by identifying skills and characteristics which will enable learners to avoid them.

The list in Table 1 overleaf is a summary of ideas and research from a wide range of sources, including course colleagues on an OET course (Certificate in Online Education and Training, London Institute of Education), a perusal of various websites and our own experience as learners and tutors in online courses. The majority of these characteristics and skills describe adult learners, rather than younger learners. In general, descriptors which refer to personality traits, often inborn, or the result of maturation (that is, more typical of adults rather than children), are called characteristics here, while skills refer to behaviours which are primarily learned. This approach has been chosen mostly for reasons of simplicity, although it is not perfectly consistent. Skills are broken down into three groups: *PC literacy/technical skills*; *language skills*, e.g. reading and writing and subskills which seem especially helpful in working online; and *metacognitive skills*, which refer to skills related to the learning process, i.e. learning about learning.

It should also be noted that this list pertains to general English language courses, and that some skills will obviously be better suited to particular skills areas.

How do students already enrolled in online English language and communication skills courses view these questions?

The British Council, Singapore organised a pilot online writing seminar for students preparing for the UCLES Certificate in Advanced English (CAE) examination. In doing so we hoped to learn three things:

- how we could utilise the British Council's bulletin board system (BBS), based on a version of Worldgroup Manager to run such courses;
- what teaching approaches and task design would work most effectively on the BBS; and
- whether online courses would actually attract students.

(As we were primarily interested in course delivery, we felt we were not yet in a position to ask the obvious question of whether online learning would improve students' scores on the written papers on the examination.)

TRAITS/CHARACTERISTICS	SKILLS
experience with distance learning	**1 Technical/computer literacy skills:**
intelligence/high ability	typing
	computer literacy
confidence/positive attitude	familiarity with online resources
maintaining self-esteem; recognizing the legitimacy of their own knowledge	**2 English language skills:**
	reading skills, including:
	the ability to read onscreen
high motivation	the ability to read and process information quickly
ability to work independently	*writing skills*, including:
	fluency: ability to write quickly
ability to collaborate with other students	awareness of audience and ability to adjust message according to one's audience
	ability to summarize one's own and other's ideas
self-discipline	ability to use appropriate register
ability to concentrate	ability to use appropriate vocabulary
	ability to use correct grammar
diligence	
willingness to ask for help	**3 Metacognitive skills:**
	ability to make critical judgements
possessing a serious attitude	ability to manage time
being 'older'	ability to monitor one's progress
	recognition of one's strengths and weaknesses
being 'mature'	understanding one's goals and objectives
	ability to reflect on what has been learned
	ability to relate what has been learned to one's own knowledge and experience
	ability to work on more than one onscreen task at once (multitasking)

Table 1 Online Skills: derived from Baker (1997); Goldman (1997); Gottschalk (1993); Hiltz (1995); Sherry (1995); Truman (1995); Turoff (1995); Wells (1995).

After this pilot version, which involved three teachers and only four students, we embarked on a larger project, called 'Write Online!', in collaboration with our colleagues at the British Council Milan. We had had an initial registration of ten students from Milan and one from Singapore.

We chose CAE writing tasks as the basis for our initial online efforts for a number of reasons:

- writing skills seemed well suited to a text-based medium, especially within the limitations of our BBS;
- an examination syllabus meant that we did not need to design an entire course; task types and marking criteria are clearly set out by Cambridge,

though in order to avoid copyright violations we used a set coursebook for some of our tasks in the pilot course and produced original materials for the second;

- CAE seemed preferable to the far more widely-subscribed First Certificate in English (FCE) examination because of the smaller number of students taking the examination; this would, we felt, make things more manageable.

Write Online! course outline

Duration: 8 weeks; each set of writing tasks took ten to fourteen days to complete.

MODULE 1: INDUCTION (1 HOUR)
Students sent messages to one another using the BBS, in order to correctly sequence a set of jumbled pictures and text.

The course outline was presented, and printed material on the use of the Worldgroup Manager software was distributed.

MODULE 2: INFORMAL LETTERS
Students were asked to exchange letters on the topic of shopping with their coursemates across the world.

MODULE 3: ARTICLES
Using information from the letters that were written and links to websites on shopping in Milan and Singapore, students produced articles on shopping in the place they didn't live in.

MODULE 4: LEAFLETS
Students wrote leaflets giving advice on how to succeed in the CAE.

MODULE 5: INSTRUCTIONS
Students were asked to write instructions for one another on how to communicate effectively in their countries.

MODULE 6: REPORT
Students were asked to write a feedback report on the course, touching on pedagogical and technical aspects of online delivery.

Teaching approaches and task design

Tasks primarily utilised one-to-many and one-to-one interaction. We tried to take advantage of the features of the BBS, which allowed us to send e-mail, set up forums (or conference groups) for different purposes, and insert HTML links to websites. The software also allowed us to change colour and fonts so that we could highlight strengths and weaknesses of students' work and send back comments which, we hoped, would be clear to them.

Where possible we tried to link tasks so that information from one could be usefully fed into another; the informal letter on the subject of shopping provided input for the subsequent article writing, for example. This in turn took advantage of the interactive capability of the BBS by getting students to acquire information from their unseen coursemates to use in their writing.

Modules were structured like face-to-face courses, with two or three pre-tasks helping to prepare students for the main writing task. We might, for example, ask students to analyse a model for cohesive devices or levels of formality, suggest headings for sections of a long text, brainstorm ideas for a text or add punctuation to a text. After submitting the main piece of writing for the module, students would be given follow-up work, usually a peer editing or assessment task.

As teachers, we could (and did) respond to students' work at any time of the day or night. Indeed, we often felt as if tutoring online was a 24-hour-a-day job. At times, there seemed to be no escape. Despite this, we enjoyed the work: the difference in approaches to writing between Italian and Asian students was refreshing and stimulating.

How did the students feel?

The difficulty of recruiting students in Singapore has already been mentioned. Only one Singaporean signed up, and so our question about recruitment was answered. When we spoke to our British Council students about this, they expressed fear of working on the computer alone at home; technophobia is not as rare as one might think on the 'intelligent island' of Singapore!

The Milan students were clearly made of sterner stuff. They were enthusiastic and hard working. Despite having to work at the British Council on a booking basis, they made most of their deadlines and impressed us. Mid-course comments on Write Online! from two of these students included the following:

• it's very useful
• it's helping me to write faster, better and more efficiently
• Singapore tutors give very prompt response, and
• it's good.

However, by the end of Write Online!, only one student remained. The same was true of our earlier pilot.

What happened?

The following comments made in the single feedback report mention similar benefits as those given above, including quick teacher feedback and the fact that learners can work in groups across the globe, but technical problems caused great frustration. These included:

• lack of technical assistance at the British Council
• frequent breakdowns in the BBS
• the need to queue for computers in the library
• the lack of a networked printer in the library, which would have enabled students to print out comments and do their editing offline.

While this information is helpful we also need to find out from our 'dropouts' why they left the course. In fact, online courses have extremely high dropout rates, as high as seventy-five per cent.

What, if anything can be done?

What recommendations can be made to ensure success in teaching and learning English online?

In this section, four areas of concern to developers of online English language courses will be discussed: learners, course design, teacher training and technical issues. The students surveyed had a high degree of confidence in the effectiveness of learning online; this level of confidence must be sustained in our courses. We need to be able to take advantage of existing skills which would ease the transition to online learning or be able to give them practice in these skills, in order to enable them to develop new skills.

Learners

Our services must be based on the needs and interests of our students, English language learners of varying ages and PC experience levels. Careful pre-course screening and induction of learners must take place, in order to ensure an adequate 'fit' between their needs and what we can offer. The following should be taken into account:

SCREENING

Students must be selected carefully, according to confidence, language skills, and computer skills and experience; they should be sufficiently mature to ask for help, and to be able to cope with technical problems without panicking. They must be convinced of the benefits of CMC to themselves as learners and willing to take a chance on trying it. They must have access to up-to-date computer equipment, whether at home, at a language centre, or elsewhere.

INDUCTION

Face-to-face meetings with other course participants and a computer orientation session should be organised before the course begins, so that, if conferencing is involved in the course, 'publishing phobia' can be avoided or at least reduced. Students will usually need to be trained in the use of the conferencing software and perhaps given instructions on how to install it at home and link it to the server.

Course design

An online course is not simply a paper course that is put onto a server, though adaptation of existing courses may be a sensible starting point for an institution about to embark on online education. If course design begins with learners' needs and interests, the following questions must be considered:

What proportion of the course will be delivered online? Additionally, which aspects of a course would be most effectively delivered online? We chose to focus on writing for the Cambridge Advanced English examination course because it was an area of need perceived both by teachers and by the learners themselves.

What software will be utilised? Software is expensive and, once in place, will have to be tolerated for a long time, if it is to be cost-effective. At the very least, interactivity, adaptability, clear interfaces, and easily accessible conferences will enable learners to come to grips with course and interpersonal issues more quickly than if they are distracted by problems with unwieldy, badly designed software. Careful research must take place before a selection is made. In our case, the selection was made for us, and both its strengths and its limitations were quickly apparent.

How should courses be organised in order to encourage participation and inter- action?   The answer to this question must be based on the aims of the course overall, of each session, and of each task, and these must be made clear to the learner from the outset. Although learning styles vary, a key factor in course success is designs which promote and sustain interaction through structured discussions and clear deadlines for tasks. These should be determined before the course begins, so that both teachers and students are clear on the work ahead. Deadlines are especially crucial for adult learners whose working and family lives require that they study asynchronously and for whom effective time management is especially important (Pincas, 1997).

To what extent should course content and design rely on the Internet?   We believe that online courses should enable learners not only to learn English language skills but also more about the Internet and the conferencing software being used. This can be done by organising tasks which require students to exchange information with each other and to access material from the World Wide Web, by inserting HTML links in postings to students.

Teacher training

Before any of the above suggestions can be carried out, familiarity with and commitment to online learning, a knowledge of its potential shortcomings and a willingness to encourage and support active learning are necessary for the instructor whose job will be to teach using CMC.

In addition, Doucet recommends 'a knowledge of a variety of educational delivery methods (including technologies). We need to have an understanding of how the technology can be applied to learning environments and how we can make the best pedagogical use of the delivery medium' (Doucet, 1997). This commitment may require changes in role:

- The online instructor must be *willing to relinquish control* of his/her 'sage on stage' role in order to allow learners to develop their own ideas and make the unique contributions which learning online can enable them to do.

- *Interpersonal and affective skills, especially when conflicts between partici- pants occur, will be essential.* In some ways, CMC robs learners of a 'human' dimension, the downside of anonymity or the 'electronic mask' Grint (1989) refers to. Some studies indicate that 'teacher mediation increases the comple- tion rate' for distance courses (Sherry, 1996); instructors will need to strike an effective balance between encouraging learner autonomy and intervening in order to maintain participation rates. Prendergast (1996) recommends the use of humour and praise and encouraging students, especially in the first few weeks, by reading and acknowledging their messages, either with praise or with a query. In our course, we also tried to follow his advice to log in every day, though we did not always succeed, as another means of allowing the 'human dimension' to filter through the typed messages which were all our Milanese students knew of us.

- Teachers will also need to be *trained in the use of the software* utilised, since courses will be run on it. They will also need to be able to acquire enough expertise to answer questions about it when students have problems, and to work with technical support staff at their institutions when necessary.

- *Being part of a team*: teachers may be team teaching large courses online for the first time, and there should be a clear allocation of roles and responsibilities and clear communication among them. Teachers may also find that *they need to consult other resource people*, including course designers, software specialists and others. This can be unsettling to those who initially went into teaching because they liked having independence and the freedom to teach as they liked. Teachers will need to understand the limits of their power, which is not an easy thing but will be rewarded by the knowledge that they can gain skills in new areas.

Technical issues

When a course is run online everyone involved is at the mercy of the system. For this reason, a number of recommendations are made:

- *Start small*: as discussed earlier, the beginning of online instruction should be made in one component of a larger course, for example, readings and comments, or the submission of written work on a writing course. This concept guided our choice in selecting CAE instead of the more popular FCE as an initial course.

- *Choose software carefully*: the issue of software, discussed in the section on course design is briefly returned to here. Assuming that choices can be made in software selection, the following suggestions are offered: a general characteristic of well accepted technology is that 'it makes a task rewarding for the user, where the "user" includes the student first, and the faculty second ... if it simplifies or expedites accomplishment of a goal, the probability of acceptance is high' (Prendergast, 1996). This highlights the need for careful scrutiny of our aims in going online, both short-term and long-term. In addition, a universal user-friendliness is necessary.

- *Skilled, responsive technical support* is essential. Loss of online time and the consequent feeling of frustration that one will never be able to catch up is a cause of reduced participation rates in CMC courses.

Conclusion

This paper has attempted to explore the reasons for success and failure of online learning by investigating available literature and evaluating a course for adult students in Singapore and Italy. In so doing it has been possible to identify some characteristics and skills of effective online learners. In order for learners to enjoy success in their English language learning, careful research and planning is required. In addition, stringent screening and teacher training should help to ensure that online education programs enjoy the success that is our goal.

Epilogue: The Fifth Paradox: What's the English Lesson All About?

Péter Medgyes
Eötvös Loránd University, Budapest

'If a man could pass through Paradise in a dream, and have a flower presented to him as a pledge that his soul had really been there, and if he found that flower in his hand when he awoke – Ay! and what then?'

Samuel Taylor Coleridge

Prelude

It was 2.30 in the morning when the doorbell rang. In pyjamas, I shuffled out to open the door. There were two men standing at the doorway. They were both wearing trench coats and hats. 'Professor Medgyes?' the shorter one asked. No sooner had I whispered 'yes' than they grabbed me, forced me down the stairs and pushed me into a big black car.

A few minutes later the car pulled up. As we got out, I saw we had stopped right outside a school building. 'Hmm! But this is Jóska!' I said to myself. The secondary school which I had attended many years before.

The building was pitch-dark. As we entered, I recognised Laci bácsi, sitting in his lodge, his face fluorescing. The wicked old porter! He would never let any boy leave the building before the day was over. There was complete silence, except for our echoing footsteps. With a metal object pressed hard against my ribs, the two men walked me up the stairs. By the time we had reached the top floor, alas, it was broad daylight.

There were hundreds of boys scurrying up and down the corridor. The clamour was unbearable. Then the bell went off, and everybody headed for their classrooms. When all the doors had closed, I was made to move on as far as the classroom at the end of the corridor.

'But this was my own classroom!' I muttered. 'Not to worry. It's an English class in there,' the shorter guy growled, tore the door open and pushed me inside.

All the students stood to attention. 'Good morning, sir,' they chanted as I stumbled in. They didn't seem to notice that I was wearing pyjamas. 'Goo...good morning,' I answered. Everybody sat down and opened their books. I had my own copy on the teacher's desk. *Blueprint Upper Intermediate* (Abbs and

Freebairn, 1993). I plucked up enough courage to ask: 'Where did we stop last time?' 'Page 9,' they answered in chorus.

I opened the book.

How daring are YOU?

Do you enjoy taking risks? Complete the questionnaire to find out.

		Yes	No
1	Have you ever tried a 'dangerous' sport like parachuting, hang gliding or scuba diving?	☐	☐
2	Do you usually catch trains, buses and aeroplanes at the last possible moment?	☐	☐
3	When trying something new, do you worry a lot about looking silly?	☐	☐
4	Do you often wear daring or unusual clothes?	☐	☐
5	Have you ever volunteered to go on stage in a theatre?	☐	☐
6	Have you ever been on a blind date?	☐	☐
7	Do you avoid dangerous rides in fairgrounds?	☐	☐
8	Do you know which are the safest seats to choose on an aeroplane?	☐	☐
9	Did you make any new friends during your last holiday?	☐	☐
10	Do you get frustrated with people who drive too slowly?	☐	☐

Check your score

1	yes 1	no 0	6	yes 1	no 0
2	yes 1	no 0	7	yes 0	no 1
3	yes 0	no 1	8	yes 0	no 1
4	yes 1	no 0	9	yes 1	no 0
5	yes 1	no 0	10	yes 1	no 0

Score analysis

If you scored between 8 and 10
You like taking risks. However, you need to remember that sometimes you have to balance risk-taking with caution and good sense.

If you scored between 4 and 7
You are sensible and realistic about the result of any risk you might take.

If you scored between 0 and 3
You are careful by nature. The trouble with having such a mature and cautious attitude is that your life may seem to be dull and boring.

'*How daring are YOU?*', read the title. A psychological test: that should be fun! 'OK, let's get going!' I said, having regained my professional confidence. But then a boy from the back shouted: 'We're fed up!'

I nearly swooned. It was myself. Péter Medgyes at the age of sixteen. 'And we were fed up with Dr G. as well. Our previous English teacher. That's why we did him in.' I suddenly felt weak in the limbs. As I turned around, I saw the two thugs towering above me, their arms crossed on their chests.

'What do you want?' I asked in dismay.

'We want you to explain the difference between anaphora, cataphora and deixis.'

'I beg your pardon?'

'Are you deaf or what? I said: Anaphora, cataphora and deixis.'

'But I can't,' I said. 'I'm not a linguist.'

'What are you then?' my alter ego demanded.

'I'm a language teacher. An English teacher.'

'And what do you know, Mr English Teacher?'

'Well, I can speak English.'

'Big deal! Billions of people can.'

'But I can teach it, too. I've been teaching English for thirty years.' ('Keep talking,' I said to myself. 'As long as you talk, they won't hurt you.') 'Of course it's not only the language I know. I've obtained information about lots of other things. May I give you a few examples?'

'Let's hear them!' said the chorus.

'Well, I know for a fact that the cheetah is the fastest animal in the world. Not the lion and not the antelope, as one would imagine, but the cheetah. It can run at a speed of 176 kilometres per hour. I also know that in 1990 Steffi Graf was the queen of tennis, and Mother Teresa was still up and running. At that time, Gorbachev was under no compulsion to pose for Pizza Hut for a paltry honorarium of one million dollars, and *Mrs* Thatcher was not yet *Lady* Thatcher. It was just one year before heavyweight champ Mike Tyson began to serve his prison sentence for having beaten up and raped his wife. Who could have predicted then that only seven years later he would bite off his opponent's ear?'

'Old hat,' young Medgyes snarled. 'That's all in Unit One, *Blueprint One.*' (Abbs and Freebairn, 1990). 'We learnt all that stuff the first day we met the late G.'

'Oh, but I know far more than *Blueprint One*. Or the whole series for that matter.' Panic helped my brain towards alpha rhythm. I felt as though I were racing down a narrow tunnel. 'I know all about famous tourist spots from the Taj Mahal to the flora and fauna of the Galapagos Islands. But I'm also well informed about the most recent technological advances and New Age matters. Biorhythms, acupuncture, aromatherapy: that's the real stuff! My mind boggles when I read about dangerous sports like hang-gliding, scuba-diving and bungee-jumping. I'm concerned about global issues: the population explosion, deforestation, the greenhouse effect, to name just a few. And when it comes to horror movies, brrr, they send shivers down my spine. Violence scares me.'

'I bet it does,' young Medgyes hissed.

'Fortunately, coursebooks supply more material on the bright side of life. Romances, soap operas, pop stars. Phew, the mere mention of the Spice Girls, Pete Sampras and Naomi Campbell makes my pulse quicken. And, like everyone else, I'm terribly fond of short snippets from here and there and everywhere. Did you know, for example, that the citizens of Kentucky, USA, are required by law to take a bath once a year? Or that in Madagascar it is illegal for pregnant women to wear hats or eat eels?' (Greenall, 1996)... 'All in all, coursebooks provide an endless source of knowledge and fun.'

'Fun, fun, fun. What if I gave you a good kick in the belly? Or knocked you unconscious? How's that for fun? These coursebooks teach you nothing, nothing worthwhile. You think very lowly of us, sir,' said the young monster as he began to move slowly towards me. 'Like Dr G., who would go to the barber's shop every morning just to have his hair combed. He needs no barber any more. Nor will you, sir.' By this time, his face had come close-up. Covered in acne. 'I will teach you not to be so patronising, sir. But the tuition fee will be expensive. Very very expensive.'

There was no time to lose. In one desperate move, I shot out of the classroom. It was pitch-dark again. I knew the building like the palm of my hand. Twenty-one steps to each flight of stairs. Taking three steps at a time, I hurtled down to the ground floor. I was no more than a few feet from the main gate when I tripped and fell flat. As I was sliding down the marble floor, I heard the high-pitched voice of Laci bácsi, the porter: 'The day is not yet over, kid.'

I hit the gate head first. Bang!

... I woke up in a sweat. I turned on the bedside light and looked at my watch. It was four-thirty in the morning. Then my eyes fell on a thick bundle of A4-size sheets in the middle of the floor. I picked it up and looked at the title page: '*Paradoxes of Language Teaching*. Written by Emil Galambos'.

As I leafed through the manuscript, I realised that it was unfinished. It ended on page 472. The text was typed on an old mechanical typewriter; the letter 's' was hardly legible and the letter 'b' was wonky throughout. At eight o'clock in the morning, I called the department secretary to tell her that I was feeling ill and would stay in bed. It took me two full days to drag myself through the turgid prose of Dr G. But it was well worth the effort. It was the most stimulating work I'd ever read. I shall try and summarise the main points of the dissertation, paradox by paradox, as far as the author got before he met his fate.

Paradox 1   The learning content vs. the carrier content

The author's first claim is that English, or any other foreign language, occupies a unique place among the school subjects. Whereas a history, chemistry or music lesson *explicitly* deals with its subject matter, a foreign-language lesson is only *implicitly* concerned with its own content, that is the Grammar of L2.

Take a geometry lesson, for example. The teacher discusses the triangle: she explains how the length of the hypotenuse can be computed given the lengths of the two sides of the right-angled triangle. Then she supplies a couple of problems to check understanding and the students' ability to apply the rule. The lesson focuses on the triangle and nothing else. There's no beating around the bush, because geometry, like any other discipline, has a direct body of knowledge that has been 'consciously acquired by scientists over years of study and that can be transmitted by conscious and overt instruction of various sorts' (Gee, 1988:218-9). Incidentally, the same applies to the so-called skills subjects.

In her environment, the foreign-language teacher sticks out like a sore thumb for she has no such explicit knowledge available. Or rather, she has two different kinds of subject matter to teach simultaneously: the Grammar of L2 and the topics which serve to carry the specific items of Grammar and demonstrate their use (Medgyes, 1994). Littlejohn (1992) calls these two sets the *learning content* and the *carrier content*.

To illustrate his point, Dr G. analyses an exercise from *New Headway Intermediate* (Soars and Soars, 1996). The learning content is *must* and *mustn't*, presented within the framework of a contextualised drill. The ensuing dialogue, below, between Mum and Jim purports to be the carrier content.

> 1   T.27a Jim is going to backpack around the world for
> a year, but his mother is worried. Listen to them.
>
> Mum   You must write to us every week!
> Jim   Yes, Mum! I will.
> Mum   You mustn't lose your passport!
> Jim   No, Mum! I won't.
>
> Work in pairs. Make similar dialogues between Jim
> and his mother. Use the cues and *must* or *mustn't*.
>
> – look after your money   – talk to strangers
> – go out when it's dark   – drink too much beer
> – make sure you eat well   – have a bath regularly
> – phone us if you're in   – go anywhere that's
>   trouble   dangerous

However, the author finds fault with this dialogue. Who are Mum and Jim? They're mother and son all right, but what's their family name? Why do they make their one and only appearance on page 37? How old is Jim? Twenty? Eighteen? Surely he hasn't cut his secondary school studies only to gallivant around the world for a whole year? Why are the learners made to eavesdrop on this silly dialogue anyway? To make them jealous of this spoilt brat, perhaps?

The dialogue is no less implausible and artificial than it is irritating, Dr G. contends. Can you imagine a mother reeling off her worries in such an inordinate fashion? Does it ever happen, except in a classroom situation, that ten warnings are followed by ten curt responses, all of them dressed up in exactly the same linguistic disguise? Moreover, Jim needn't even grasp the meaning of Mum's words to be able to supply the right response; all he has to know is that *must* should be acknowledged with *Yes, Mum! I will* and *mustn't* with *No, Mum! I won't*, throughout the drill.

The author draws the conclusion that in drills the carrier content is a mere excuse for highlighting the learning content. Dad could substitute for Mum and Julie for Jim without altering the pattern. The cues provided could be replaced by others, and the whole situation could be metamorphosed into something completely different. Anything on earth will do so long as it serves as a linguistically adequate context for the presentation and practice of *must* and *mustn't*. Teachers who give priority to the learning content may be called *formalists* (Rivers, 1981).

In contrast, *activists* are preoccupied with the carrier content. They are led by the belief that one can best learn something by rehearsing it in real-life situations. Therefore, the teacher's main job is to give her students every opportunity to use L2 as a genuine means of communication. The formal properties of the language should be taught only to the extent that they help the learners convey their message.

This line of thought has a familiar ring to it, doesn't it? It is communicative language teaching.

The activist, alias the communicative teacher, puts forward three propositions:
- learners have messages to convey
- the foreign language is a genuine means of communication for learners
- the foreign-language lesson is suitable for creating real-life situations.

The author's critique is aimed at these three propositions. Let me summarise his rambling thoughts one by one.

Paradox 2 Learners have NO messages to convey

To repeat, foreign languages are unique subjects. While other subject teachers talk business, the foreign-language teacher is engaged in an endless stream of pseudo-talk. The students next door strive to comprehend the general theory of relativity, discuss the significance of the French revolution or listen to Beethoven sonatas. Meanwhile, the English teacher asks: 'In your view, who should Alice go to the disco with: Bruce or Jason?'

This kind of sham communication is elicited by coursebooks which offer no more than a ragbag of disparate bits of information. Dr G. argues that contemporary ELT books are imitations of teenage magazines, featuring the same columns and the same light-hearted topics. In a word, they are glitzy junk.

As for coursebook writers, most of them are unscrupulous business people, who go out of their way to pander to the taste of every potential customer from the Kuril Islands down to Patagonia. As a result, their products are clones of one another. Teachers take their pick or get hooked by the book promoter with the sweetest tongue.

'But why do we let all this rubbish fill our schools?' Dr G. asks. And his answer is: 'Because we are too weak to block the flood. We live in an Augean stable [...] Heracles, where are you?' he exclaims at the end of some fifty pages of convoluted moralising.

Needless to say, coursebooks are mere tools for communicative missionaries to spread their beliefs. One such creed is that language learning is all laughter and merriment. It's like TV channel-hopping or pulling the lever of the one-armed bandit.

Another misconception is that the English lesson has its own areas of study beyond and above the teaching of linguistic signs. During its ruthless reign, communicative language teaching has foiled any attempt to bring Grammar back into the classroom. Naturally enough, the communicative dogma has been invented by native teachers who seldom excel as grammarians.

Nowadays, says Dr G., most teachers in the ELT village are suffocating, but few dare to speak up. But the real victims are the students. In the beginning, they trust that by the time they leave school, they will have mastered the English language. Weeks, months and years go by and their command of English is still minimal. Sooner or later, the less persistent simply write off English as another wasted subject in the curriculum, whereas more mature students begin to give voice to their frustration. Like the following adult group.

After the students had read an article about homeless people in Britain, they were asked to compare them with the homeless in their own country. For some reason, the discussion just wouldn't pick up steam and it soon creaked to a halt. The teacher's reaction was to reproach the students for the fiasco. Then he accused the article of failing to arouse interest. The circumstances were not very favourable either, he thought; it was the sixth lesson that day, everybody was exhausted. Deep down, however, he put most of the blame on himself. Noticing his anguish, one of his students stepped up to him after the class and said: 'Look, it's not your fault. The thing is we never talk about such issues. Not even in Hungarian. Why don't you try and teach us the English language instead?'

The lesson to learn from this story is that learners have no specific messages to convey. As such. They come to the English class simply to learn the Grammar of English. They don't need the pill sugared. They are not the weaklings that the commissars of the communicative doctrine would have us believe. As long as they see the language point, they are ready to enter into a discussion on any issues: homeless people or multi-millionaires; issues they take no specific interest in and have no specific views on; even issues which they wouldn't normally reveal in public, let alone in a foreign language.

The lack of a relevant message explains why teachers generally pay little heed to the carrier content. They take their students' utterances at face value: contextualised language practice. Like the teacher in the following story.

Once he was presenting the *what make?* structure to a group of eleven-year-olds. He asked the pupils: 'What make is your parents' car?' 'It's a Ford', 'It's a Volkswagen', 'It's a Trabant', the children eagerly replied. After the lesson, one of the boys stepped up to him and happily announced that they had just changed their Trabant for a Nissan. The teacher stared at him vacantly, but gradually it dawned on him that the boy had taken a mechanical drill for a real enquiry (Medgyes, 1994).

Dr G. closes this chapter with a subtle metaphor. Teachers and learners, he says, have to be made aware that grammatical items can't run amok naked. They always put on a robe. This robe may be one hundred per cent silk or one hundred per cent polyester, or any combination of the two materials. The quality of the material is obviously not beside the point, nor is the couture. But at the end of the day it's what's beneath the robe that matters: the body.

Paradox 3 The foreign language is NOT a genuine means of communication for learners

In the previous chapter, the author claimed that learners have nothing to say in the English lesson. In this chapter, he argues that even if they should have a message, English or any other foreign language is not an appropriate tool to convey that message.

First he reminds us that every teacher is a language teacher, and the study of any subject is essentially the study of language. In biology, mathematics, or history, the teacher's primary job is to teach a way of talking and, therefore, seeing the world (Postman and Weingartner, 1969). Language is the most direct way of passing information about most disciplines, and even in the case of 'skills subjects', language is an important go-between. It goes without saying that the natural vehicle of communication is the mother tongue throughout the curriculum.

The relationship between language and knowledge is respectively that of the means and the end. Here again, the foreign-language teacher is the odd man out or, indeed, the odd *woman* out. For her, L2 embodies both the means and the end (Antier, 1976). Typically, she teaches knowledge *about* and skills *in* L2 mediated by the same foreign language (Breen, 1985), except when she calls on the mother tongue for help in monolingual settings.

In contradiction to the proponents of communicative language teaching, Dr G. believes that learning a foreign language is a painful process. Learners wage a war of attrition, and the vast majority lose out on at least two counts. Namely, they will never be able to express themselves in L2 at a level adequate (a) to their intellectual potential, and (b) to their mother-tongue competence. No matter how hard they try. A sense of underachievement appears to be the concomitant of learning a foreign tongue – and a source of constant disappointment.

Language lessons deal heavy blows on the learners' ego. As long as they practise linguistic features within the narrow confines of drills and traditional exercises, they can manage. However, the moment they are obliged to use L2 as a medium of 'genuine communication', the intellectual level of their performance drops. Harder claims that:

> to be a wit in a foreign language you have to go through a stage of being a half-wit – there is no other way (Harder, 1980:269).

A protracted process, says Dr G. For many learners, it takes forever.

Adult learners are particularly upset as they perceive their self-esteem fraying at the edges, and many of them:

> get into a state of 'psychic death' in the foreign language class as they feel they are losing the ego established with so much pain during their lives (Bárdos, 1984:116).

The psychologically less balanced often throw in the towel or get counted out. Those with more stamina set various defence mechanisms in motion.

In sum, Dr G. argues that L2 is *not* a genuine means of communication in the foreign language class. Every sentence uttered is unworthy of the learners' intellectual capability. No one can perform as articulately and as naturally in L2 as in their mother tongue. Sadly enough, this also applies to non-native teachers. For all intents and purposes, classroom interaction has a false ring to it. Dr G. agrees with Naimann *et al.* that:

> While first-language competence is compelling and self-evident, many features of the new language are arbitrary, artificial, unnatural and sometimes finicky, fussy, and often plainly ridiculous (1977:13).

Or as Kosztolányi (1922), a prewar Hungarian writer, put it:

> When I first heard foreign speech in my childhood, I had a good laugh. Flotsam and jetsam. Toy words. I still remember that laugh. Yes, only my mother tongue is the real one, the serious language. All the rest in which I often read, and sometimes even speak, are bird languages' .

Paradox 4 The foreign-language lesson is NOT suitable for creating real-life situations

Dr G. maintains that the foreign-language lesson is not suitable for creating real-life situations. Whatever a real-life situation means... Indeed, what does it mean? How is a real-life situation different from a classroom situation? The author registers five distinguishing features (borrowed, as it happens, from Medgyes 1995).

- Real-life communicative situations are induced by real communicative needs which the partners wish to satisfy. Such exigencies seldom exist in the classroom.
- The scope of real-life situations is impossible to delimit, since they encompass the full spectrum of human activities. In contrast, classroom situations may be designed with a high degree of precision.
- Real-life situations are complex and closely interrelated; acoustic, visual, tactile and olfactory sensations are in harmony with intellectual and affective components. In the classroom, these networks are loose and random.
- Real-life communicative situations are linguistically rich: registers embrace an area far wider than would be necessary or feasible for classroom use.

• The errors made in the classroom have no grave consequences – compared to those committed in the outside world.

The author hastens to admit, though, that the classroom is also a segment of the world. It is, to quote Littlewood:

> a real social context in its own right, where learners and teacher enter into equally real social relationships with each other (1981:44).

Thus it is more apt to assume a hierarchical rather than a mutually exclusive relationship between real-life and classroom situations.

Returning to the differences, Dr G. quotes Byrne:

> Why is it so difficult to teach a foreign language? To a large extent, it is because we are attempting to teach in the classroom what is normally – and perhaps best – learnt outside it (1976:1).

Nunan (1987) goes even further by suggesting that the outside world just cannot be brought into the classroom. Classroom activities designed to simulate real life are bound to be contrived, often to the point of absurdity.

To illustrate this incongruity, the author borrows an anecdote from my treasure trove. Many, many years ago, I happened to be teaching two nine-year-olds, a girl and a boy. In one of the first lessons, I was presenting the prepositional phrases: *in, on, under.* To illustrate the difference, I put a book alternately in the desk, on the desk and under the desk. Before long, the boy began to chuckle. 'What's up?' I asked. 'But sir, can't you see where the book is?' The little girl snapped at him, 'Come on, of course he can! He's just trying to teach us the new words.' Unlike the boy, then, the girl had already understood the intrinsic absurdity of life in the classroom.

In further analysing this issue, Dr G. refers to Pearse (1983), who makes a distinction between *realistic* and *real* communicative situations. Whereas in a realistic situation we say something in order to use the language, in a real situation we use the language in order to say something.

But is it possible to create real situations in the classroom? It depends, Dr G. says. Teachers are in a double bind. On the one hand, they intend to develop skills that help students get by in the classroom. Basically, this job involves the teaching of classroom language ('Hey, spit out that chewing gum, will you?'; or 'But we were supposed to do the test next week – not today!'; or 'Put your tongue between your teeth. Now say: "th".') (Medgyes, 1985). Now in the classroom, these utterances *do* have face value – they *are* real.

On the other hand, teachers are also, and mainly, obliged to enable students to use L2 in communicative situations *outside* the classroom. This is an infinitely trickier task! Such encounters range from the immediate to the far away. For instance, in an immediate situation the student, upon leaving the school building, may be asked the way by a foreigner; in a distant situation the student-turned-scientist may deliver a lecture at an international conference. In either case, however, the classroom does not easily lend itself to authentic practice.

In the language lesson, the teacher can undertake no more than to *rehearse* language skills which will be called for in real-life communicative situations –

perhaps, sooner or later. Krashen (1982) says that learning in the classroom is a transitional pursuit. That is true, but what isn't transitional, Dr G. asks?

But the worst news is yet to come. In a monolingual setting, the rehearsals are usually conducted by the non-native teacher; a person with a deficient command of the foreign language; the blind leading the blind. The teacher and her students share the same mother tongue, yet they use L2 most of the time. Isn't it odd?

In quest of the fifth paradox

With Paradox 4, the bulky manuscript came to an end. An abrupt end, I should add. Let me quote the last paragraph from page 472:

> Strangely enough, none of the paradoxes on which I elaborated in the preceding chapters have thus far been discussed in the literature. Nobody has pondered upon these dilemmas at any length. [...] It is high time for us to get out of the rut and rectify the situation. In the concluding chapter, therefore, I shall advance a fifth paradox, which is destined to crack all the problems of language teaching.

However, no sooner had the phoenix begun to flutter his wings than it was shot down...

I was left in a state of agitation. For the next four days, I racked my brains in the hope of finding the fifth paradox Dr G. had had no time to put forward. However, I failed to make any progress whatsoever. I gradually sank into apathy. I unplugged the telephone and let the blinds down. And then, on the fifth day, a ray of early morning light pierced its way through the blinds. It fell upon a book on my bookshelf. I struggled to my feet and took the book off the shelf. It was a specimen from my collection of old ELT books. A textbook written for secondary school pupils in the last year of their studies (Fest *et al.*, 1942). It was marked with a purple stamp: 'Vida Book and Stationery Company, Makó (next to the *Gimnázium*)'. The book fell open on pages 46 and 47.

The facing pages (shown opposite) contained a photograph of Christ Church College, Oxford, a couple of seventeenth century poems, and a cavalier to match. And on the margin, lo and behold, the signatures of Dr G., Dr Emil Galambos, in several variations.

Who could have put them there? Could it have been a schoolgirl who was in love with Dr G., her young teacher; or G. himself, still a student? Was he practising his autograph in the idle moments of the English lesson; a young man brash enough to grant himself the title of doctor well in advance?

Stuck between those two pages, I found a yellow scrap of paper. The following stanza was scribbled on it in indelible pencil:

> Until you leave,
> Until the end,
> Suspend, my friend,
> Your disbelief.

Who could have written this four-liner? Could it have been a Restoration poet? That is unlikely. Or was it the girl in love, or G., while preparing for his exams?

TOM TOWER, CHRIST CHURCH COLLEGE, OXFORD
One of the most characteristic buildings of the «Cavalier Capital»

Quit, quit for shame! This will not move;
    This cannot take her.
If of herself she will not love,
    Nothing can make her.
    The devil take her!

To a Girl, on Going to the Wars

Richard Lovelace (1618—1658)

Tell me not, Sweet, I am unkind
    That from the nunnery
Of thy chaste breast and quiet mind,
    To war and arms I fly.

True, a new mistress now I chase,
    The first foe in the field;
And with a stronger faith embrace
    A sword, a horse, a shield.

Yet this inconstancy is such
    As you too shall adore;
I could not love thee, dear, so much,
    Loved I not honour more.

A CAVALIER OF THE RESTORATION

Of Human Life

Henry King (1592—1669)

Like to the falling of a star,
Or as the flights of eagles are, —
Or like the fresh spring's gaudy hue,
Or silver drops of morning dew;
Or like the wind that chafes the flood,
Or bubbles which on water stood:
Even such is man, whose borrowed light
Is straight called in, and paid to night.
The wind blows out, the bubble dies;
The spring entombed in autumn lies;
The dew dries up, the star is shot;
The flight is past — and man forgot.

To Daffodils

Robert Herrick (1591—1674)

Fair daffodils, we weep to see
    You haste away so soon:
As yet the early-rising Sun
    Has not attain'd his noon.
    Stay, stay,

'Suspend, my friend, your disbelief.' No, it's far too sophisticated for an eighteen-year-old. But it could be *Dr* G., the teacher, couldn't it? Yes, why not? 'Suspend your disbelief.' It sounds like him, doesn't it? It has the same bombastic touch. It can't not be Dr G.! I've got it! I've found the fifth paradox; the key to the whole caboodle... Emil, you've saved my life. May you rest in peace!

I ran to the windows and pulled up the blinds. The sun struck me hard, but then I flicked on the computer and frantically jotted down the fifth paradox.

Paradox 5 Suspend your disbelief!

Before I let you into Paradox 5, let me summarise the main points we have dwelt on so far. According to the four paradoxes, learning a foreign language in the classroom is a most peculiar activity. In terms of their content, language lessons run at two levels, but these two levels are so intricately interwoven that they are virtually impossible to disentangle.

Learners do not come to the foreign-language class to obtain and convey information, and the artificial nature of the classroom does not stimulate genuine interaction, either. To make matters worse, learners' attempts at free communication are hindered by their language deficiencies.

On the credit side, learners are prepared to engage in any kind of interaction provided it helps them acquire the Grammar of L2. It also has to be admitted that the language class is a suitable environment for rehearsing the foreign-language skills which will be required outside the classroom.

Altogether this is not a very rosy picture, is it? And yet, billions of people, young and old, learn foreign languages the world over. They stammer and stutter, take ages to blurt out sentences which only make sense if enormous quantities of goodwill are exercised by native speakers. Learners are constantly humiliated by their ineptitude, which is exposed in a cage called the classroom.

Nevertheless, most of them persist and drag along – for years, for decades, for a whole lifetime. What gives learners the stamina to persevere and rise from their ashes day after day? How come they are prepared to make a fool of themselves at every turn of the foreign-language class? They are obviously propelled by the desire to master the foreign language. The urgency of short-term, medium-term and long-term goals is far too evident to beg detailed justification. But surely there is more to it than motivation alone. The answer is simple – and this is Paradox 5:

> Language learning is an occupation which calls for a suspension of disbelief.

Let me explain what I mean. The foreign-language classroom is a world in its own right. The moment you hop on this merry-go-round, you are obliged to shed your real identity. For forty-five or fifty minutes, you are neither the pauper, nor the prince. You are a child turned into an adult, or an adult turned into a child. In either case, you wear the cap and bells. You act and roleplay and sing and dance and do the splits and somersaults. As a newly adopted member of a crazy family, all you need to do is watch the others and follow the ground rules. It won't take long to realise that nothing is real here, everything is simulated. It is a world turned upside down: abnormality is the standard norm.

To survive in this weird segment of the universe, you have to cast aside all your doubts and act on trust – unconditional trust that you place in your teacher, the Grand Inquisitor, to use Stevick's (1980) term. Entering into this voluntary bondage will relieve you of any feeling of remorse and distress. There you stand, naked, unashamed before your teacher.

Trust works wonders with the learning process. The only snag is that it is fragile. Handle with care. Trust is not to be abused – as Dr G. did.

What do you mean, I hear you ask? Well, he put on the communicative cap although he was a formalist at heart. He played this double game in order to be in line with the ruling methodology. Soon enough, however, his students saw through Dr G. 'He is a hypocrite, unworthy of our trust,' they grumbled. The spell was broken – and so was his neck in the end. It was a sad lesson for teacher education!

But let me finish on a happier note. Language learning is a game (Berne, 1964). Or rather, it is a farce. It is not to be played with a straight face, unless it is deadpan, like Buster Keaton. Good language lessons are rife with tongue-in-cheek remarks, euphemisms, understatements and inverted commas. Jokes are dispensable – humour is not. Humour should permeate every niche of the class-room – and self-irony! Let's all look in the mirror, open our hearts and laugh at our follies (Naimann *et al.*, 1977).

Coda

The next day I went back to work, lithe and alert. My colleagues gave me a searching glance. 'You don't look like someone who was ill in bed for a fort-night,' they said.

Nowadays, every night as I turn off the bedside lamp, I wish the bad dream would haunt me again. The second act. If only I could tell young Medgyes, 'Listen! I've found out the secret. The key to language teaching. And I'm the only person in the world who knows the secret.'

Well, not the only one. You readers, you know it as well now.

'That willing suspension of disbelief for the moment, which constitutes poetic faith.'

Samuel Taylor Coleridge

Acknowledgments
I would like to thank Valéria Árva, Jozefa Kamondi and Christopher Ryan for their comments and suggestions.

Bibliography

Abbs, B. and Freebairn, I. (1990) *Blueprint One* London: Longman.

Abbs, B. and Freebairn, I. (1993) *Blueprint Upper Intermediate* London: Longman.

Aitken, A.J. (1985) 'Is Scots a language?' in *English Today* 3, 41-5.

Alderson, J.C. and Beretta, A. (eds) (1992) *Evaluating second language education* Cambridge: Cambridge University Press.

Amato, P. and Snow, M. (1992) *The multicultural classroom* London: Longman.

Ambrose-Yeoh, A. (1997) 'Distance education and in-service language teacher development' in Hayes, D. (ed.), 86-98.

Antier, M. (1976) 'Language teaching as a form of witchcraft' in *English Language Teaching Journal* 31/1, 1-10.

Armitage, S. and Bryson, M. (1997) 'Using Lotus Notes for asynchronous collaborative learning and research' OET document, London: Institute of Education.

Baker, I. (1997) 'Re: Any questions?', OET document, London: Institute of Education.

Bárdos, J. (1984) 'Az idegen nyelvek tanítása a '80-as években' [The teaching of foreign languages in the 80s] *Pedagógiai Szemle* 34/2, 105-118.

Barmada, W. (1994) 'Developing an institutional self-evaluation scheme in an ESP Centre in the Arab world: rationale, experimentation and evaluation', unpublished PhD thesis, Department of Linguistics, University of Leeds.

Barnes, D. and Todd, F. (1977) *Communication and learning in small groups* London: Routledge.

Baskaran, L. (1994) 'The Malaysian English mosaic' in *English Today* 37, 27-32.

Baxter, A. (In process) 'The reproduction of professional culture through teacher education for ELT', unpublished paper, Department of Language Studies, Canterbury Christ Church University College.

Beaumont, M. and Wright, T. (1998) 'ELT and paradigm shifts: in from the cold or out on a limb', unpublished paper presented at the IATEFL conference, Manchester.

Berge, Z. and Collins, M. (1995) 'Computer-mediated communication and the online classroom: overview and perspectives' in *Computer-Mediated Communication*, 2/2.

Berne, E. (1964) *Games People Play: The Psychology of Human Relationships* Harmondsworth: Penguin Books.

Biederstädt, W. (1993) *Materialen für Bilinguale Klassen, vol. 1: Around the World* Berlin: Cornelsen-Verlag.

Binns, L.S. (1998) 'Topic work as a vehicle for the teaching of English as a foreign language in a private Turkish Cypriot primary school: action research in the classroom', unpublished M.Ed. dissertation, University of Nottingham.

Bird, N. *et al.* (eds) (1993) *Language and content* Institute of Language in Education: Hong Kong.

Bowers, R. and Widdowson, H. (1986) 'A debate on appropriate methodology' in Abbott, G. and Beaumont, M. (eds) *The Development of ELT: the Dunford Seminars 1978-1993*, ELT Review, Hemel Hempstead: Prentice Hall and the British Council 141-5.

Breen, M.P. (1985) 'The social context for language learning – a neglected situation?' in *Studies in Second Language Acquisition* 7/2, 135-158.

Brewster, J. (1992) 'Language across the curriculum: from policy to practice' in Skehan, P. and Wallace, C. (eds) *Thames Valley University Working Papers in English Language Teaching* 1, 60-87.

Brewster, J., Ellis, G. and Girard, D. (1991) *The primary English teacher's guide* Harmondsworth: Penguin Books.

Brown, A. (1978) 'Knowing when, where and how to remember: a problem of metacognition' in Glaser, R. (ed.) *Advances in instructional psychology* Hillsdale, N.J., Erlbaum.

Buchanan, D. and Boddy, D. (1992) *The expertise of the change agent* London: Prentice Hall.

Byrne, D. (1976) *Teaching oral English* London: Longman Group Limited.

Cameron, D. and Leung C. (1998) 'Research interest group news' in *NALDIC News* 14, 17-19.

Cameron, L., Moon, J. and Bygate, M. (1996) 'Language development of bilingual pupils in the mainstream: how do pupils and teachers use language?' in *Language and Education* 10/4, 221-236.

Child, J. (1984, 2nd edition) *Organization: a guide to problems and practice,* London: Paul Chapman.

Clark, J. (1987) *Curriculum renewal in school foreign language learning* Oxford: Oxford University Press.

Clark, R. and Ivanic, R. (1997) *The politics of writing* London: Routledge.

Claxton, G. (1990) *Teaching to learn: a direction for education* London: Cassell Educational Ltd.

Clegg, J. (ed.) (1994) 'Language and cognition in second-language-medium education: how English as a second language is taught in British mainstream classrooms' in *Triangle* 13 Goethe Institut/British Council/Ens-Credif: Diffusion Didier-Erudition: 131-139.

Clegg, J. (1996) *Mainstreaming ESL* Clevedon: Multilingual Matters.

Cohen, A., Weaver, S. *et al.* (1995) 'The impact of strategies-based instruction on speaking a foreign language' Minnesota, National Language Resource Center, University of Minnesota.

Coleman, H. (ed.) (1996) *Society and the language classroom* Cambridge: Cambridge University Press.

Collier, V. (1994) 'Plenary address, TESOL Conference' reported by Olson R. *et al*, in *TESOL Matters* 4/3.

Corson, D. (1990) *Language policy across the curriculum* Clevedon: Multilingual

Matters.

Crooks, T. and Crewes, G. (eds) (1995) *Language and development* Bali: IALF.

Crystal, D. (1995) *The Cambridge Encyclopedia of the English Language* Cambridge: Cambridge University Press.

Crystal, D. (1996) 'The past, present and future of English rhythm' in Vaughan-Rees, M. *Changes in Pronunciation*, IATEFL Pronunciation Special Interest Group, Summer Newsletter 8-13 Whitstable: IATEFL.

Crystal, D. (1997) *English as a global language* Cambridge: Cambridge University Press.

Crystal, D. (1998) 'The future of English: where unity and diversity meet', keynote address to TESOL Arabia, Al Ayn, March.

Cummins, J. (1981) 'The role of primary language development in promoting educational success for language minority students' in California State Dept. of Education (ed.) *Schooling and language minority students: a theoretical rationale* Los Angeles: California State University.

Cummins, J. (1984) *Bilingualism and special education: issues in assessment and pedagogy* Clevedon: Multilingual Matters.

Dam, L. (1995) *Learner Autonomy 3: From theory to classroom practice* Dublin: Authentik.

Dam, L. and Legenhausen, L. (1996) 'The acquisition of vocabulary in an autonomous learning environment – the first months of beginning English' in Pemberton, R. *et al.*, 265-280.

Department for International Development (1998) Draft Education Policy Paper quoted in DEVLANG-L, British Council on-line discussion forum.

Department of Education and Science (1975) *A Language for Life* ('Bullock Report') London: HMSO.

Dickinson, L. and Carver, D. (1980) 'Learning how to learn: steps towards self-direction in foreign language learning in schools' in *ELT Journal*, 35/1, 1-7.

Dörnyei, Z. (1994) 'Understanding L2 motivation: on with the challenge!' in *Modern Language Journal*, 78/4, 515-523.

Doucet, M. M. (1997) 'Re: Developers and deliverers', OET document, London: Institute of Education.

Dunford Seminar Report (1989) *Managing ELT Aid Projects for Sustainability*, British Council.

Dunford Seminar Report (1990) *Training for sustainability of ELT aid projects*, British Council.

Eastment, D. (1996) *The Internet and ELT: The impact of the Internet on English language teaching* British Council, London.

Ellis, G. and Brewster, J. (1991) *The storytelling handbook for primary teachers* Harmondsworth: Penguin Books.

Ellis, G. and Sinclair, B. (1989) *Learning to Learn English – A Course in Learner Training – Learners' Book* Cambridge: Cambridge University Press.

Faerch, C. and Kasper, G. (1983) *Plans and strategies in interlanguage communication* London: Longman.

Fairclough, N. (1995) *Critical discourse analysis: the critical study of language* London: Addison Wesley Longman.

Fest, S., Országh, L., Szenczi, M. and Berg, P. (1942) *Angol Nyelvkönyv, Book 4* [English textbook] Budapest: Franklin-Társulat.

Flavell, J.H. (1970) 'Developmental studies of mediated memory' in Reese, H.W. and Lipsitt, L.P. (eds) *Advances in child development and behaviour* New York: Academic Press.

Flavell, J.H. (1976) 'Metacognitive aspects of problem solving', in Resnick, L.B. (ed.) *The Nature of Intelligence* Hillsdale: N.J. Erlbaum.

Flew, A. (1995) 'Counterpart training and sustainability: effecting an exchange of skills' in Crooks, T. and Crewes, G. (eds) 76-82.

Frühauf, G., Coyle, D. and Christ, I. (1996) *Teaching content in a foreign language* Alkmaar: European Platform for Dutch Education.

Fullan, M. (1991) *The new meaning of educational change* London: Cassell.

Galloway, I. (1996) 'Computer-mediated communication in second/foreign language teaching', unpublished paper, University of London Institute of Education.

Gardner, R.C. and MacIntyre, P.D. (1991) 'An instrumental motivation in language study: who says it isn't effective?' *Studies in Second Language Acquisition* 13, 57-72.

Gardner, R.C. and Tremblay, P.F. (1994) 'On motivation: measurement and conceptual considerations' in *Modern Language Journal* 78/4, 524-7.

Gee, J.P. (1988) 'Dracula, the Vampire Lestat and TESOL' in *TESOL Quarterly* 22/2, 201-225.

Genesee, F. (ed.) (1994) *Educating second language children* Cambridge: Cambridge University Press.

Gibbons, P. (1991) *Learning to learn in a second language* Newtown NSW Australia: Primary English Teaching Association.

Goldman, S.S. (1997) 'Re: Any questions?' OET document, London: Institute of Education.

Gottschalk, T. (1993) 'Strategies for learning at a distance' Guide 9, adapted from Willis, B. (1993) *Distance education: a practical guide* Englewood Cliffs, NJ, USA: Educational Technology Publications.

Graddol, D. (1997) *The future of English* London: The British Council.

Green, J.M. and Oxford, R. (1995) 'A closer look at learning strategies, L2 proficiency, and gender' in *TESOL Quarterly* 29/2, 261-297.

Greenall, S. (1996) *Reward Upper-Intermediate* Oxford: Heinemann English Language Teaching.

Grint, K. (1989) 'Accounting for failure' in Mason, R. and Kaye, A. (eds).

Harasim, L. (1989) 'On-line education: a new domain' in Mason, R. and Kaye, A. (eds).

Harder, P. (1980) 'Discourse as self-expression – on the reduced personality of the second-language learner' in *Applied Linguistics* 1/3, 262-270.

Harri-Augstein, S. and Thomas, L.F. (1991) *Learning conversations; the self-organised learning way to personal and organisational growth* London: Routledge.

Hawkins, E. (1984) *Awareness of language: an introduction* Cambridge: Cambridge University Press.

Hayes, D. (1997a) 'INSET, innovation and change: an introduction' in Hayes, D. (ed.) 1-7.

Hayes, D. (1997b) 'Articulating the context' in Hayes (ed.) 74-85.

Hayes, D. (ed.) (1997) *In-service teacher development: international perspectives ELT Review* London: Prentice Hall.

Heindler, D. (1996) 'Forms of bilingual education in Austria' in Frühauf, G., et al. 13-30.

Heuring, C. and Zhou, R. (1995) 'Distance learning strategies in China: using the strategy inventory for language learning to compare distance and classroom learners in China' in Hong Kong Polytechnic University: *Working Papers in ELT and Applied Linguistics* 1/2, 95-110.

Hiltz, S.R. (1995) 'The virtual classroom', paper presented at the 1995 International Conference on Computer Assisted Instruction, National Chiao Tung University, Hsinchu, Taiwan.

Hofstede, G. (1991) *Cultures and organisations: software of the mind* Maidenhead: McGraw-Hill.

Holec, H. (1981) *Autonomy and foreign language learning* Oxford: Pergamon.

Holliday, A.R. (1994) *Appropriate methodology and social context* Cambridge: Cambridge University Press.

Holliday, L. (1997) 'The grammatical quality of e-mail messages by international EFL/ESL students on the Internet', paper presented at the First Pan-Asia conference and 17th Annual Thai TESOL International Conference, Bangkok.

Hooper, H. (1996) 'Integrating science with a majority of ESL learners: integrating language and content' in Clegg, J. 217-236.

Jacob, G. (1996) *The CDS co-ordinator* unpublished paper, Department of English, University of Pune, India.

Jarvis, J. (1996) 'Using diaries for teacher reflection on in-service courses' in Hedge, T. and Whitney, N. (eds) *Power, pedagogy and practice* Oxford: Oxford University Press, 150-162.

Jarvis, J. and Cameron, L. (1997) 'Role shifting in INSET: an exploration of a primary English project' in Hayes, D. (ed.) 37-49.

Jones, B.A., Palinscar, A. *et al.* (1987) *Strategic teaching and learning: cognitive instruction in the content areas* Alexandra, Va.: Association for Supervision and Curriculum Development.

Kenny, B. and Savage, W. (eds) (1997) *Language and Development: teachers in a changing world* London: Longman.

Kelly, R. (1996) 'Language counselling for learner autonomy: the skilled helper in self-access language learning' in Pemberton, R. *et al.* 93-113.

Kiely, R. (1996) 'Professional development for teacher trainers: a materials writing approach' in *ELT Journal* 50/1, 59-66: Oxford: Oxford University Press

Knowles, E. (ed.) (1997) *The Oxford Dictionary of New Words* Oxford: Oxford University Press.

Kolodziejska, E. *et al.* (1997) 'Towards common principles of foreign language learning' Report of the First Network Meeting, European Centre for Modern Languages, Graz: Council of Europe/WSIP.

Kosztolányi, D. (1922) *Pesti Hírlap*, 13 January.

Kramsch, C. (1993) *Context and culture in the language classroom* Oxford: Oxford University Press.

Krashen, S.D. (1982) *Principles and practice in second language acquisition* Oxford: Pergamon Press.

Kuchl, I. and Simpson, S. (1995) *English across the curriculum series: great changes* Vienna: OBV Paedagogischer Verlag.

Lawrence, P.R. and Lorsch, J.W. (1967) *Organization and Environment: managing differentiation and integration* Boston, MA: Harvard University, Graduate School of Business Administration.

Leppänen, S. and Kalaja, P. (1995) 'Experimenting with computer conferencing in English for Academic Purposes' in *English Language Teaching Journal* 49/1, 26-36, Oxford: Oxford University Press.

Little, D. (1991) *Learner autonomy 1: definitions, issues and problems* Dublin: Authentik.

Littlejohn, A.P. (1992) 'Why are English language teaching materials the way they are?' unpublished manuscript, Lancaster: Lancaster University.

Littlewood, W. (1981) *Communicative language teaching* Cambridge: Cambridge University Press.

Long, M. and Porter, A. (1985) 'Group work, interlanguage talk and second language acquisition' in *Working Papers* 4/1, 103-137, Department of ESL, University of Hawaii.

Lunzer, E. and Gardner, K. (1984) *Learning from the written word* Edinburgh: Oliver & Boyd.

Marland, M. (1977) *Language across the curriculum* London: Heinemann.

Martin, W.M. and Balabanis, L.P. (1995) 'Team development in ELT projects: a case study' in Crooks, T. and Crewes, G. (eds) 16-30.

Mason, R. and Kaye, A. (eds) (1989), *Mindweave*, Pergamon Press, Oxford.

McArthur, T. (1998) *The English Languages* Cambridge: Cambridge University Press.

McGroarty, M. (1992) 'Co-operative learning: the benefits for content-area teaching' in Amato, P. and Snow, M. (eds) 58-69.

Medgyes, P. (1985) *Classroom English – Osztály, vigyázz!* Budapest: Tankönyvkiadó.

Medgyes, P. (1994) *The Non-Native Teacher* Basingstoke: Macmillan Publishers.

Medgyes, P. (1995) *A kommunikatív nyelvoktatás* [Communicative language teaching] Budapest: Eötvös József Könyvkiadó.

Medgyes, P. (1997) *A nyelvtanár* [The language teacher] Budapest: Corvina.

Mercer, N. (1995) *The Guided Construction of Knowledge* Clevedon: Multilingual Matters.

Met, M. (1994) 'Teaching content through a second language' in Genesee, F. (ed.) 159-182.

Middleton, J., Rondinelli, D. and Verspoor, A. (1987) *Designing Management for Uncertainty and Innovation in Education Projects* Washington, DC: World Bank.

Mintzberg, H (1979) *The Structuring of Organizations: a synthesis of the research* Englewood Cliffs, NJ: Prentice-Hall.

Mohan, B. (1986) *Language and Content* Don Mills, Ontario: Addison-Wesley.

Mohan, B. (1993) 'A common agenda for language and content integration' in Bird *et al.* (eds) 4-19.

Montgomery, M. (1998) 'What is British Cultural Studies anyway and why are people saying such terrible things about it? in *British Studies Now* 10, 3-6.

Moore, M. (1991) 'Distance education theory' in *The American Journal of Distance Education* 5.3.

Moore, S. (1998) 'Real Britannia: what does it mean to be British?' *The Independent (Monday Review)*, 20 January 1998.

Mort, Simon (ed.) (1986) *Longman Guardian New Words* London: Longman.

Naimann, N., Fröhlich, M., Stern, H.H. and Todesco, A. (1977) *The good language learner* Ontario Institute for Studies in Education.

Newby, D. (1997) 'Establishing principles and guidelines for publishers and authors of FL textbooks in the context of the aims of the ECML' in Kolodziejska, E. *et al.* (eds) 1-34.

Nisbet, J. and Shucksmith, J. (1986) *Learning Strategies* London: Routledge

Nunan, D. (1987) 'Communicative language teaching: making it work' in *ELT Journal* 41/2, 136-145.

Nunan, D. (1991) *Language Teaching Methodology* London: Prentice Hall.

Nunan, D. (1997) 'Strategy training in the language classroom: an empirical investigation' in *RELC Journal* 28/2, 56-81.

O'Malley, J.M., Chamot, A.U., Stewner-Manzanares, G., Kupper, L, and Russo, R.P. (1985a) 'Learning strategies used by beginning and intermediate students' in *Language Learning* 35/1, 21-46.

O'Malley, J. M., Chamot, A.U., Stewner-Manzanares, G., Russo, R.P. and Kupper, L. (1985b) 'Learning strategy applications with students of English as a second language' in *TESOL Quarterly* 19, 285-296.

O'Malley, J.M. and Chamot, A.U. (1990) *Learning Strategies in Second Language Acquisition* Cambridge: Cambridge University Press.

Oxford, R. (1990) *Language learning strategies: what every teacher should know* Rowley, Mass.: Newbury House.

Paulsen, M.F. (1995) 'Learning activities for electronic distance education' online discussion, International Conference on Distance Learning, Birmingham.

Pearse, R. (1983) 'Realistic and real English in the classroom' in *English Teaching Forum* 21/3, 19-22.

Pemberton, R., Li, E.S.L., Or, W.W.F. and Pierson, H.D. (eds) *Taking control: autonomy in language learning* Hong Kong: Hong Kong University Press.

Pennycook, A. (1994) *The cultural politics of English as an international language* London: Addison Wesley Longman.

Pernet, D. (1996) 'Bilingual education in France, the European sections' in Frühauf, G. *et al.* 67-79.

Phillipson, R. (1992) *Linguistic imperialism* Oxford: Oxford University Press.

Pincas, A. (1997) 'Why computer conferencing may help students more than face-to-face teaching' OET document, London: Institute of Education.

Postman, N. and Weingartner, C. (1969) *Teaching as a subversive activity* London/New York: Penguin Books.

Prendergast, G. (1996) 'Re(2): Planning', OET document, London: Institute of Education.

Ravindran, R. (1998) 'En route to learner independence via learning conversation and language counselling' in Renandya, W.A. and Jacobs, G.M. (eds) *Learners and Language Learning* Singapore, SEAMEO Regional Language Centre, Anthology Series 39, 56-71.

Rivers, W.M. (1981) *Teaching Foreign-Language Skills* Chicago: The University of Chicago Press.

Rondinelli, D.A., Middleton, J. and Verspoor, A.M. (1990) *Planning Education Reforms in Developing Countries: the contingency approach* Durham, NC: Duke University Press.

Rosen, B. (1994) 'Is English really a family of languages?' in *International Herald*

Tribune, 15 October 1994.

Sherry, L. (1996) 'Issues in distance learning' in *International Journal of Distance Education*, 1/4, 337-365.

Sinclair, B. and Ellis, G. (1992) 'Survey: learner training in EFL coursebooks' in *ELT Journal*, 46/2, 209-225.

Smith, H. (1995) 'Power and sustainability in language-related development projects' in Crooks, T. and Crewes, G. (eds) 65-75.

Smith, H. (1997) 'Donors and recipients' in Kenny, B and Savage W. (eds) 208-217.

Smith, H. (1998) 'Perceptions of success in the management of aid-funded English language teaching projects' PhD thesis: University of Reading.

Smith, N.L. (1991) 'Evaluation reflections: the context of investigations in cross-cultural evaluations' in *Studies in Educational Evaluation*, 17, 3-21.

Snow, M., Met, M. and Genesee, F. (1992) 'A conceptual framework for the integration of language and and content instruction' in Amato, P. and Snow, M. 27-38.

Soars, L. and Soars, J. (1996) *New Headway English Course Intermediate* Oxford: Oxford University Press.

Stevick, E.W. (1980) *Teaching language: a way and ways* Rowley, Mass.: Newbury House.

Stoller, F. (1994) 'Diffusion of innovations in intensive ESL programmes' in *Applied Linguistics* 15/3, 300-27, Oxford University Press.

Swain, M. (1995) 'Three functions of output in second language learning' in Cook, G. and Seidlhofer, B. (eds) *Principle and practice in applied linguistics* Oxford: Oxford University Press, 125-144.

Swales, J. (1980) 'The educational environment and its relevance to ESP programme design' in *Projects in Materials Design*, ELT Documents Special, London: The British Council, 61-70.

Tang, G.M. (1992) 'The effect of graphic representation of knowledge structures on ESL reading comprehension' in *Studies in Second Language Acquisition* 14, 177-195.

Taylor, G. (1997) 'Management issues in INSET: a practical perspective' in Hayes, D. (ed.) 116-127.

Thorley, P. (1994) *Integrating language and content in the national curriculum: the knowledge framework approach in Year 7 Geography* Hounslow: Hounslow Language Service.

Truman, B. (1996) 'Distance education in post secondary education and business since 1988' available FTP: http://pegasus.cc.ucf.edu/~btruman/dist-lr.html.

Turoff, M. (1995) 'Designing a virtual classroom' paper presented at 1995 International conference on computer assisted instruction, National Chiao Tung University, Hsinchu, Taiwan.

Ukraine Project Teams (1997) *Baseline Studies* (unpublished).

Usher, R. and Edwards, R. (1994) *Postmodernism and education: different voices, different worlds* London: Routledge.

Verspoor, A (1985) *Project Management for Educational Change* Washington, DC: World Bank.

Vygotsky, L.S. (1978) *Mind in society; the development of higher psychological processes* Cambridge, MA: Harvard University Press.

Wall, D. (1996) 'Introducing new tests into traditional systems: insights from general education and innovation theory' in *Language Testing* 13/3, 334-54.

Weir, C.J. and Roberts, J. (1994) *Evaluation in ELT* Oxford: Blackwell.

Wells, G. and Chang-Wells, G.L. (1992) *Constructing knowledge together* Portsmouth NH: Heinemann.

Wells, R. (1995) 'Computer-mediated communication for distance education: an international review of design, teaching, and institutional issues' (Research Monograph 6), University Park, Pennsylvania: American Center for the Study of Distance Education.

Wenden, A. L. (1985) 'Facilitating learning competence: perspectives on an expanded role for second-language teachers' in *Canadian Modern Language Review* 41/6, 981-90.

Wenden, A.L. and Rubin, J. (1987) *Learner strategies in language learning* Prentice Hall Europe ELT.

Widdowson, H. (1978) *Teaching language as communication* Oxford: Oxford University Press.

Wong-Fillmore, L. (1985) 'When does teacher talk work as input?' in Gass, S. and Madden, C. (eds) *Second Language Acquisition* Rowley, Mass.: Newbury House.

Wong-Fillmore, L. (1989) 'Teaching English through content: instructional reform in programs for language minority students' in Esling, J. (ed.) *Multicultural education and policy: ESL in the 1990s* Toronto: Ontario Institute for Studies in Education, 125-143.

Wray, D. and Lewis, M. (1997) *Extending literacy* London: Routledge.